THE EYES
OF TEXAS
TRAVEL
GUIDE

Gulf Coast Edition

© Cordovan Corporation, Publishers
Houston 1977

Compiled and edited by the news
department of KPRC-TV, Houston

THE EYES
OF TEXAS
TRAVEL
GUIDE

GULF COAST EDITION

with a comprehensive map of the
Texas Gulf Coast, page 202

By Ray Miller

THE EYES OF TEXAS TRAVEL GUIDE
Gulf Coast edition
Ninth printing October 1979

Library of Congress Catalog Card Number: 77-15808
ISBN 0-89123-061-0
    0-89123-062-9 pbk

Cover design by Chuck Burkhardt and Russell Jumonville
Maps by Dean Nottestad

Contents

Foreword

There is much to say about Texas. It goes off in so many directions that its scenic wardrobe is of all colors and shapes. There is our heritage, our architecture, our industry old and new, and all the many, human off-the-beaten-path scenes of Texas life that make us a privileged segment of our nation.

I considered these things when Ray Miller of the "Eyes of Texas" program asked me to contribute some thoughts to this book. At first I was hesitant since this is a first time for me in this narrative direction.

Yet I do so since Ray and I through the years have shared a deep mutual interest in this big state and its vast perimeters, measurable in terms of not merely miles but history, people and delightful geography.

I know from my life in Texas how this state can affect us all. This was brought home to me recently when I went to Kerrville to view a segment of the "Eyes of Texas" with some of my staunch Texas friends. It was a good half hour and included a moving series of episodes that were close to me and my environment. And I remembered another such vignette from my past: visiting at the home of Mrs. Lizzie Ward of Mountain Home to take spinning lessons. She was one of the great masters of weaving and her work, as reflected later on the television program, brought back and helped me retain treasured memories.

So it was with another episode I well recall, when the Channel 2 cameras recorded a cattle drive from Bay City to Matagorda. This struck close to home for me since, as a teenager, I went on many cattle drives just for the fun of it. Now in later life I see this movement of men and livestock as more than fun. It is a living reflection of our heritage and, captured on film, will give later generations an insight to the forces and the people who built the state.

This book will, I hope, be another equally effective dimension by which these places and people may be captured forever so that all who come after us can see and explore what we have known. It's my personal wish that the "Eyes of Texas" has a long stand and will continue to unravel the past and explore the present. It, like this book, should focus our minds and our travels on a true enjoyment of one of the truly unique states of this great nation.

Buck Schiwetz

Introduction

Texas does not have a Coast Highway, but there is a reasonable facsimile. You can drive from Sabine Pass to Freeport with the Gulf in sight most of the way.

State Highway 87 runs between Sabine Pass and Port Bolivar. The Highway Department Ferry crosses Galveston Bay, and Seawall Boulevard will take you to FM 3005 and on into Freeport. State Highway 35 travels close to the water from Palacios to Aransas Pass. There is a free ferry from Aransas Pass to Port Aransas and a road from there down Mustang Island to the northern end of Padre Island. There is a road paralleling the coast for a short distance on the lower end of Padre Island, but there is no link between the roads at the upper end and the lower end of Padre Island. The only practical way for the average motorist with the average motor vehicle to travel between the northern and southern ends of Padre Island is inland on U. S. 77.

But we have not designed this book to follow any particular road. We have chosen to divide it into sections, and we have

included in each section some history and some points of interest that might be visited within a period of one or two days.

We have not been able to include every point of interest. It is not possible, either, to thank everybody we should thank individually. But we are indebted to the *Handbook of Texas;* the Texas Highway Department; The Texas Historical Commission; The Texas Historical Foundation; The Rosenberg Library of Galveston; the Fort Bend County Historical Museum; the Sam Houston Regional Library; to Miriam Partlow, the author of "The Atascocita District;" and to individuals all over the state for information we have used in this book and in the television program "THE EYES OF TEXAS."

RAY MILLER, GARY JAMES & BOB BRANDON

Houston, Texas

October 1977

DEDICATION

To the television audience

for encouraging us to

put into this form some of

what we have learned

from producing "THE EYES OF TEXAS"

for Texas television stations.

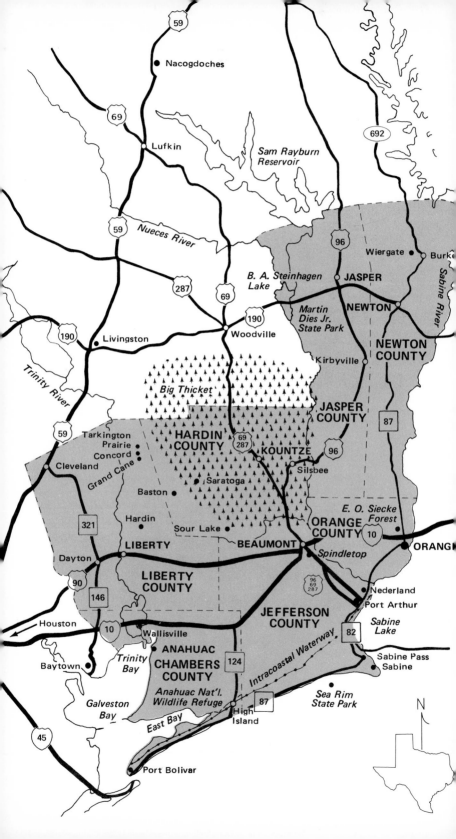

The Atascosito District and Sabine Pass

Liberty, Chambers, Hardin, Jefferson, Orange, Newton and Jasper counties

The southeastern corner of Texas is famous for oil, timber, rice, cattle and history. The early settlers here had a big hand in bringing about the revolution that freed Texas from Mexico.

France and Spain claimed this area at various times and sometimes at the same time. France claimed it was part of Louisiana. Spain said it was part of Mexico.

Neither nation did very much about it or with it during the first 200 years after their explorers learned it was here. The Spanish had a few scattered missions in the territory. And in the 1750s, the Spanish established a settlement at Atascosito Springs, just east of the Trinity River. This became the seat of what the Spanish called the Municipality of Atascosito. It included most of the present Jasper, Newton, Orange, Jefferson, Hardin, Liberty and Chambers counties, as well as Tyler, Polk and San Jacinto.

The Atascosito Road passed through here carrying traffic from the Spanish presidio at Goliad to the Sabine River and beyond. It was one of the most important and heavily travelled roads in the area during the years leading up to the revolution.

The United States bought the Louisiana Territory from France in 1803 and inherited the French claim to Texas. Spain resisted U.S. efforts to extend the U.S. border to the Rio Grande, and there was an agreement in 1818 that the boundary between U.S. and Spanish territory would be the Sabine River.

There was some movement of settlers from the United States across the Sabine. But they didn't get much encouragement until the Mexicans won their independence from Spain and started

1

1) *This marker establishes the site of Atascosito, a Spanish settlement established in 1757, designed to block French trade with the Indians. Through this area passed much of the overland traffic between Louisiana and the raw new 'Texian' frontier, prior to the Texas Revolution.*

offering liberal inducements to new settlers. It was a policy that was to cost Mexico the whole territory, and the Mexican government realized it, but not in time to prevent it.

Several Anglo families were already established in the Atascosito District by the time Stephen F. Austin got his colonization grant in 1821. The first formal census in the Atascosito District of the Mexican State of Coahuila and Texas in 1826 placed the population at 407. That figure included 76 slaves. It apparently did not include Indians. The Indians in the area were mostly Alabamas and Coushattas. They were friendly and probably too peaceful for their own good. This was one frontier where the settlers did not spend much time fighting Indians.

The name of the Municipality was changed in 1831 when Mexican Land Commissioner Francisco Madero arrived to give official approval to the colonists' land grants. Madero held an election to choose the seat of government for the District. The colonists chose the Smith Plantation, a little south of Atascosito. Madero laid out the townsite, and he and the settlers agreed to name it Libertad, or Liberty.

The name was prophetic. The residents of the Municipality of Liberty challenged the authority of an apparently over-zealous Mexican official named Bradburn at Anahuac just 13 months later. And that started the chain of events that led to the Declaration of Independence in 1836.

2

2) Stephen F. Austin, called The Father of Texas, got his colonization grant from Mexico in 1821, setting in motion the events which made Texas the Southwest outpost of English-oriented America. He died in December 1836, only a few months after Texas won independence from Mexico. 3) Early photo of an Alabama tribe member. Peaceful and cooperative, the Alabamas and Coushattas posed no threat to early colonists.

3

1) Sam Houston, the strong controversial character who commanded victorious Texan troops at the Battle of San Jacinto, also dominated Texas politics for nearly three decades. He was the new Republic's first president, later served another term, helped steer Texas into the Union in 1845. Houston was elected governor on the eve of the Civil War, refused to back secession, left office when Texans voted to join the Confederacy.

2

2) The Sam Houston Regional Library and Research Center contains a wide variety of antiques and artifacts that show the style and character of early Texas life, including 3) Sam Houston's bed.

3

4) *One of the Sam Houston Library's valued historical relics is this journal of the famed privateer, Jean Laffite. Its last entry, dated 1850, indicates Laffite did not sail into oblivion in the 1820s. This journal supports the theory that he moved to South Carolina under an assumed name. He may have circulated reports of his death as a cover.*

LIBERTY COUNTY

The government of the Republic of Texas started organizing Texas into counties shortly after it took office in 1836. Liberty County was one of the original counties. The city of Liberty has been the county seat from the beginning. Interstate 10 misses the county completely. But U. S. 90 passes right through the city. Liberty is more than 200 years old, if you count from the time the Spanish first established Atascosito. And Liberty historian Charles W. Fisher Jr. says only one other county in Texas has had as many courthouses as Liberty County. Fisher counts seven of them. The first three were timber and quickly outgrown. The fourth courthouse was brick. A fire destroyed it and most of the county records in 1874. Another brick courthouse was built in the late 1870s and torn down in 1895. That one was replaced by a typical 1890s Texas courthouse that was torn down 30 years later and replaced by the typical 1930s Texas courthouse that stands today on the same plot of ground Commissioner Madero designated for the government building in his original 1830 city plan.

Many historical documents and artifacts are on exhibit in the new Sam Houston Regional Library and Research Center. The Center is just north of the original Atascosito settlement on Farm Road 1011, north of Liberty. It was built with money raised by the Atascosito Historical Society on land donated by former Governor Price Daniel. It is operated by Lamar University. The Center has a big collection of Indian artifacts, early Texas home furnishings, pictures and paintings. One of the documents on display is the journal of the privateer Jean Laffite. It was bought and donated by Price Daniel. The Sam Houston Regional Library and Research Center is open 8 a.m. to 5 p.m., Mondays through Saturdays.

1) *Bois d'arc* trees of great age still stand near the Houston home in Liberty County. 2) *The Concord Baptist Church included among its founders Sam Houston's wife and her mother. Services are still conducted here.*

William Barrett Travis and Sam Houston both practiced law in Liberty. There is a marker on the building that now stands where Sam Houston's law office stood, at the corner of Main Street and Sam Houston Avenue.

Houston had two homes in Liberty County. He had a small log cabin on a large tract at Cedar Point, where Cedar Bayou empties into Trinity Bay. He used the place as a summer home until he

3) Plantation Ranch, restored and operated by Bill Daniel, preserves many buildings as they appeared when Texas' Trinity River carried boat passengers and freight to and from early settlements.

died in 1863. Houston retired to Cedar Point briefly after he was forced out of the Governor's office in 1861 for opposing secession from the United States. The house is no longer standing. The site is in what is now Chambers County, near Cove off Farm Road 2354. Houston and his wife, Margaret, also had a home 23 miles north of Liberty on the east side of what is now State Highway 146. There was a river settlement called Grand Cane here then. No trace of the settlement is left today, except the bois d'arc trees the settlers imported to provide their chickens with a place to roost, safe from possums, coons and foxes. The bois d'arc trees have tough thorns on the trunks. They are not native to this part of the state.

Mrs. Houston and her mother were founding members of the Concord Baptist Church. The church is about six miles north of Grand Cane, and services are still conducted here, but the building is not the original one. The church is situated on a country road that runs west toward the Trinity from State Highway 146. Joseph and Benjamin Ellis were also founding members of the Concord Baptist Church. They were the original owners of the riverfront plantation later restored and now operated by Bill Daniel. The Trinity carried most of the passengers and freight to and from the ranches and settlements before the railroads came. Historian Miriam Partlow lists 98 steamboats known to have operated on the Trinity between 1838 and 1878. A barge canal serves

1) This early photo of a Texas river steamer shows the crowds and commerce that moved on inland waterways in the 19th Century. 2) For his aid to desperate early pioneers, Chief Kalita of the Coushatta Tribe is remembered with this memorial between Liberty and Concord. He gave food and help to settlers fleeing from Santa Anna's Mexican Army in 1836.

Liberty today, and some Dallas interests still dream of a series of locks to make the river navigable all the way to north Texas.

A monument on State Highway 146 about halfway between Liberty and Concord honors the early Coushatta Indian Chief Kalita. He furnished food and help to many of the settlers fleeing toward the Louisiana border during the Runaway Scrape, when it appeared Santa Anna's army was going to wipe out the revolutionary forces.

The Wells General Store, built in 1875, still stands in Tarkington Prairie. This community was founded by Barton Tarkington in 1827. It was the first settlement in the county, west of the Trinity River.

One of the earliest major Texas cattle producers was James Taylor White. He operated a spread from headquarters situated southeast of Liberty in what is now Chambers County. Jones and Company of England established on the banks of the Trinity at Liberty the first commercial meat packing plant in Texas.

Several homes from the late Nineteenth Century are still standing on the older streets in Liberty.

3) The steamboat Horatio, in this 1894 photo, is docked just south of where the US 90 bridge now spans the Trinity River. 4) A few Texas longhorns may still be seen at Liberty County ranches. 5) The Abbott-Parker home, Liberty. 6) The T. J. Chambers home, Liberty.

1) Cattle and oil today play major roles in the economy of Chambers and other coastal counties. Imported Brahman and Charolais cattle have been crossed onto domestic breeds here with excellent results. 2) This is one of the more typical views along the Texas Gulf Coast: barbed wire, a "stock tank" for cattle, and an oil drilling rig prospecting for new energy supplies.

A party of French exiles led by General Charles Lallemand set up a base near the present town of Liberty in 1818. Lallemand and his followers had been supporters of Napoleon Bonaparte. They fled after Waterloo, and their apparent intention in settling in Texas was to establish a base for a Bonaparte revival. They called their base on the Trinity River Champ d'Asile. They pretended to be settlers, but they were heavily armed.

Napoleon's brother, Joseph, was living in New Jersey. Historians believe Lallemand and his followers planned a campaign to free Mexico from Spain, put Joseph Bonaparte on the throne of Mexico, and then rescue Napoleon from St. Helena. Contemporary Spanish and U. S. authorities thought the same thing. Spain sent an expedition from Mexico to attack Champ d'Asile, but Lallemand and his party had scattered by the time the Spanish arrived. The Spanish burned the settlement and the log fortifications, and nothing is left at the site today except the marker the State of Texas put up in 1936. The marker is on the south side of U.S. 90, near the east bank of the Trinity.

3) *The lure of fishing poles and freshwater streams is strong to many travelers in Texas and they leave the freeways to prospect along secondary roads, such as this highway near Anahuac. 4) A rusting anchor marks the site of Old Fort Anahuac, founded in 1821. It is now a state park.*

4

CHAMBERS COUNTY

Chambers County was formed in 1858 from parts of Liberty and Jefferson counties. The original county seat was Wallisville on the Trinity. It was moved to Anahuac in 1908. The present courthouse was built in 1935. It was the first air-conditioned courthouse in Texas. All of Trinity Bay and much of Galveston Bay lie within the Chambers County boundaries. Oil, cattle and rice are the big moneymakers in Chambers County.

Interstate 10 cuts across the north part of the county. It misses the county seat of Anahuac where the history is concentrated. The Spanish established a fort at Anahuac in 1821. The site is now a park. This was a point of entry for settlers from the United States under the Spanish and Mexican administrations. The Mexicans had a man named Juan Bradburn in charge at Anahuac in 1831. He had a series of disputes with the settlers, and he jailed William Barrett Travis during one of those disputes. Other settlers persuaded Bradburn's superior to depose Bradburn and free Travis. During this exercise, the colonists drafted what

11

1) William Barrett Travis, called the Hero of the Alamo, once was jailed by a political opponent in Anahuac. In 1835 he raised a company of volunteers to capture the Mexican garrison then holding Anahuac. 2) Here the Turtle Bayou Resolutions were drafted, putting Mexico on notice that the Texas settlers were impatient with their political position.

3) Thomas Jefferson Chambers, after whom the county was named, was lawyer, judge, soldier and a major early landholder.

came to be called the Turtle Bayou Resolutions, protesting the policies of the Bustamente government in Mexico City and calling for a return to the Mexican Constitution of 1824. The Turtle Bayou Resolutions were the first formal notice that the settlers in Texas were growing impatient with their status. A state marker at White Ranch Park on I-10, six miles northeast of Anahuac proclaims this as the place where the resolutions were drafted.

The Chambers County Historical Commission has preserved two historic buildings on a site adjacent to the Chambers County Courthouse on Washington Avenue at Cummings in Anahuac. The Thomas Jefferson Chambers home was built here in 1838. Chambers called it Chambersia.

Thomas Jefferson Chambers was born in Virginia. He came to Texas by way of Mexico. He studied Mexican law there, and when he came to Texas he was Surveyor General for the government of the Mexican State of Coahuila and Texas. He was also designated superior judge for the territory, and he held several large Mexican land grants. The present State Capitol at Austin stands on land the Mexican government granted to Chambers, and the State finally paid Chambers' heirs $20,000 for it in 1925, 60 years after Chambers was assassinated as he sat in his home at Anahuac.

1) This office of pioneer Texas physician Nicholas Schilling has been preserved as a museum. It is located alongside 2) the Chambers House at Anahuac. It was here that Thomas Jefferson Chambers lived, and where he died from the bullet of an unknown assassin.

Chambers sided with the colonists in their dispute with the Mexican government. He played a major role in the Revolution, and he was commissioned a major general in the Texas Army Reserve. Chambers County was named for him.

The home Chambers built at Anahuac has a window with the panes arranged like the Lone Star of Texas. Somebody fired a shot from outside one day and killed General Chambers as he was sitting in an upstairs room. There is a story that the bullet passed through Chambers' body and hit a portrait of him. The bullet

3) *The depths of the Big Thicket in many places are inaccessible and seldom seen by outsiders. Giant cypress trees produce odd "knees" that grow to the height of a man. Here, Naturalist Lance Rosier examines some of the largest in the Thicket.*

supposedly hit the painted figure in the same spot it hit the general himself in. The shooting occurred in 1865. The gunman never was found.

There are no regular hours, but you can visit the home any time you can find somebody in the County Clerk's office free to show you through.

The office of Dr. Nicholas Schilling was moved to the site alongside the Chambers home from Cedar Bayou where Dr. Schilling worked until he died in 1919. Schilling was born in Germany. The Schilling family donated the office to Chambers County complete with all the equipment, medicines and records Dr. Schilling left in it when he died.

The Anahuac National Wildlife Refuge is on East Bay, south of Farm Road 1985. It is open to visitors. There is no charge.

HARDIN COUNTY

The Big Thicket is not as big as it once was, but it is still the biggest thicket in Texas, and much of what is left of it is in Hardin County.

1) Hardin County's relatively new courthouse (1958) contrasts sharply with many of the stately, highly ornamented courthouses built in Texas in the late 19th Century. Many ornate courthouses and valuable early records have been destroyed by fires over the years.

The county was formed in 1858 from parts of Liberty and Jefferson counties. It was named for five brothers, Augustine, Benjamin, Milton, Franklin and William Hardin. They were early and prominent settlers in Liberty County.

A town was established to be the county seat. It was also named Hardin, but the Sabine and East Texas railroad laid its tracks so as to miss Hardin by a couple of miles. The railroad promoters were two brothers named Kountze. They established a new town beside their tracks and named it for themselves. Railroad promoters did that a lot. Hardin went into a decline. The courthouse there burned in 1887, and the county seat was then moved to Kountze. The present courthouse was built in 1958. Kountze is on U. S. 69 between Beaumont and Woodville.

Timber is one of the principal resources of Hardin County, and the sawmill town of Silsbee is the commercial center. Timber magnate John Henry Kirby built his first sawmill in Silsbee in 1896. Silsbee is in the eastern end of the county where State Highway 327 meets Farm Road 92.

The oldest town in Hardin County is Sour Lake. It may be a long time before the Arabs get the price of oil as high as it was in Sour Lake in the last half of the Nineteenth Century. Oily water used to sell here for 50 cents a glass. People came to Sour Lake to drink it for their health, before they discovered some of the other things it is good for. The oily water oozed out of the ground. Stephen Jackson is credited with founding the town and discovering that people would pay money to drink the oily water. A black man known as Dr. Mud is said to have made a fortune shipping it to customers outside of Texas. A fashionable hotel was built on the lake in 1851, and many rich and famous people came here to bathe and drink the water. Sam Houston was here in 1863 shortly before he died. The hotel eventually burned, and people quit drinking the water when commercial oil development started.

 2

2) *Sour Lake before the turn of
the century was a busy, growing
town, fueled in part by a wide-
spread belief that its oozing, oily
waters had medicinal value. For
some years, it was a spa of considerable note and prominent
people came to drink the waters
and take the baths. 3) When serious oil drilling began in Sour Lake
it caused a boom of staggering
dimensions and literally covered
the landscape with oil rigs. In the
1920s a large section of this land
area caved in, burying derricks
and equipment.*

3

The first big gusher here came in in 1902. It was here that the
company that became the giant Texaco organization got its start.
There was no regulation of oil production in those early days.
Speculators and promoters flocked into Sour Lake. The population soared from 40 to 20,000 in four months, and oil derricks
covered the landscape.

1) These celebrants at a "Roundup" in Batson testify to the free-wheeling exuberance of the early oil boom towns that flourished, then faded, in the early 20th Century.

Nothing remains of the old health spa at Sour Lake, but there are a few old wooden storage tanks from the early days of the Sour Lake oil boom. Sour Lake is at the southern end of Hardin County where State Highway 105 and State Highway 326 meet.

Tiny Batson had an oil boom about the same time as Sour Lake. The population here grew from a few dozen to 10,000 almost overnight. Batson had a reputation as one of the rowdiest towns in Texas for a brief period when the new hotels and saloons were overflowing with oilmen, but it is quiet again today. Batson is on the western edge of Hardin County, where Farm Road 770 and Farm Road 162 meet.

Saratoga was named for the famous New York resort because this Saratoga also enjoyed a brief reputation as a health resort, after J. F. Cotton discovered some medicinal springs here. Commercial oil development began at Saratoga about 1901, and people lost interest in the springs.

There are several opinions about where the boundaries of the Big Thicket are, but Saratoga is well within the Thicket by just

2

2) It is possible now to drive deep into many areas of the Big Thicket on relatively good roads. Ornithologists and plant lovers consider it one of the nation's finest refuges for wildlife and growing things.

about any definition. The town has long been headquarters of the Big Thicket Association. It is situated where State Highway 105 meets Farm Road 770.

A fair idea of what is left of the Thicket can be obtained from any of the roads and highways in this part of Hardin County. The great stands of longleaf pine that once characterized the Thicket have been turned into lumber. Still standing though are oaks of a dozen varieties, magnolia, gum, ash, maple, beech, hickory, cypress, persimmon and mulberry trees, holly, chinquipin, plum, dogwood, yaupon and palmetto. Several varieties of orchid grow in the Thicket, too.

Some people have claimed they have seen ghostly lights at night along the old road between Saratoga and Bragg. This road is uncommonly straight because it follows an old railroad line. The forest grows close on both sides. The lights may be just swamp gas, but that possibility has not prevented the road from becoming known as the Ghost Road.

1) *The Spindletop oil strike put Beaumont on the map and this busy port helps keep it there. Along with its traffic in oil, sulphur — loaded along the Neches — is a major recent ingredient in the port's business.*

JEFFERSON COUNTY

Jefferson was one of the original Texas counties established by the government of the Republic in 1836. It was organized in 1837 with Beaumont as the county seat. The county was named in honor of U. S. President Thomas Jefferson. The city of Beaumont had been founded by Henry Millard in 1835 on land he bought from early settler Noah Tevis. The city may have been named for Millard's friend Jefferson Beaumont, or it may have been taken from the French term for a small hill near the townsite. That's never been settled.

Beaumont is a major port on the Neches River. It is on Interstate Highway 10, and it is the most industrialized and urbanized part of the old Atascosito-Liberty District. Spindletop made Beaumont one of the earliest oil boom towns. Petroleum remains one of the principal industries here, and the Beaumont-Port Arthur-Orange complex today serves and supports and profits from the growing offshore oil operations in the Gulf.

Rice is a major crop in Jefferson County and the upper coastal region. The first rice was planted here in the 1850s. The Port Arthur Canal Company began cultivating rice with irrigation in the 1890s. A marker on the Beaumont Rice Mill testifies that it was the original Texas rice mill.

The Jefferson County Courthouse in Beaumont was built in 1931.

2

2) As this Beaumont mill attests, rice has long been a major crop in Jefferson and adjacent counties. 3) The French Homestead, built in 1845 by an early Beaumont settler, has been preserved by the local heritage society.

One of the oldest buildings in Beaumont is the trading post and homestead built in 1845 by John Jay French. French was a tanner as well as a trader, and he was determined to be a frontiersman. He moved on from here to far west Texas because Beaumont very early got too crowded for him.

The Beaumont Heritage Society maintains the French Homestead, and it is open to the public from 1 to 4 p.m. Tuesdays through Sundays. The French Homestead is at 2995 French Road, just off Delaware Street, on the west side of Beaumont. There is a small charge for admission.

1

1) Famed in many a movie and novel, this is how the most spectacular of all the early day gushers — the Lucas well at Spindletop — actually looked as it spewed oil on January 10, 1901. Upshot of this event was the creation of new oil companies and the early beginnings of America's huge industrial expansion, powered by petroleum.

Spindletop

Oil had been discovered elsewhere earlier, but the oil industry in Texas really got its start at Spindletop outside Beaumont on January 10, 1901. A promoter named Padillo Higgins had formed the Gladys City Oil, Gas and Manufacturing Company nine years earlier. Higgins planned to discover oil in the salt dome at Spindletop and use the money to build a dream city. Mining engineer Anthony Lucas took over the operation in 1889. He made two or three attempts to complete a well and then called in the Hamils of Corsicana to take over the drilling. The drillers were actually changing bits that January morning in 1901 when the oil and gas erupted through the bottom of their hole and exploded into the biggest gusher anyone had seen anywhere up to that time.

The boom that followed helped create the Gulf Oil Company and several other major petroleum companies. There is a derrick and a granite monument today at the site of the Lucas gusher on Spindletop Avenue, on the southeastern city limits of Beaumont.

The boomtown that grew up around the Spindletop Oil Field bore little resemblance to the city Padillo Higgins had dreamed of. It was thrown up in haste; flimsy frame buildings lining muddy streets. The real Gladys City vanished a long time ago, like most of the other boom shantytowns. But the Beaumont Bicentennial Commission built a replica of Gladys City on the campus of Lamar Tech, on Cardinal Drive, near the site of the Lucas

2

3

2) Gladys City, the boomtown that grew up around the original Spindletop oil field, has been rebuilt as a Beaumont museum on the campus of Lamar Tech. 3) The Babe Didrikson Zaharias Center is a memorial to the famous woman athlete who won Olympic honors then many golf championships.

gusher. It is a museum where as many artifacts from the Spindletop era as can be found will be preserved. Gladys City is open to the public from 1 to 5 p.m., Sundays through Thursdays; and 9 a.m. to 5 p.m. on Saturdays. It is closed Fridays. There is a small admission fee.

One of the world's greatest athletes grew up and got her start in Beaumont. Babe Didrikson was a basketball star in school. She took up track and field events, qualified for the 1932 Olympics and broke two women's world records there. She later married wrestler George Zaharias and took up golf. She won 36 tournaments in four years and was the first American to win the British Women's Amateur Championship. Babe Zaharias died of cancer in 1956 at the age of 45 and she is buried in Forest Lawn Memorial Park in northeast Beaumont. The Babe Didrikson Zaharias Center on Interstate 10 houses momentoes and the trophies she won. It is open every day and free.

1) Beaumont's Tyrell Historical Library is a repository for important information and exhibits that give the history and lifestyle of early Southeast Texas settlers.

The Geology Department of Lamar University operates a Spindletop Museum on U. S. 90 west of Interstate 10. It features a half-hour movie about Spindletop narrated by Walter Cronkite, and it is open from 1 to 4 p.m. daily except Mondays.

The Tyrell Historical Library in the old First Baptist Church Building at 695 Pearl contains much valuable information about the early history and the early settlers of this area. The library is closed Sundays and Mondays. It is open Thursdays from noon to 9 p.m., and Tuesdays, Wednesdays, Fridays and Saturdays from 10 a.m. to 6 p.m. More information about sights and events in Beaumont can be obtained from the Visitor Information Center, I-10 at Walden exit.

U. S. Highway 69-96-287 connects Beaumont with Port Arthur and passes by Nederland. Some of the first settlers after this town was founded were people of Dutch descent. Some of the descendants of the original Dutch settlers still live here. They have a replica of a Dutch windmill on the main street. It is a combination museum and gift shop. Wooden shoes from the old country are among the big items here. The windmill was built by the Nederland Chamber of Commerce in 1969. It is said to be an exact replica of mills actually used in Holland, but the blades on this one are turned by an electric motor. The interior is air-conditioned, and the artifacts on display are not all Dutch. Some belonged to the late country music star Tex Ritter. He claimed Nederland as his home town. The Windmill Museum is open Thursday through Sunday afternoons. Admission is free.

Nederland also had a number of settlers of Cajun background. These were descendants of French settlers dispossessed by the British when they took over the Maritime Provinces of Canada. Many of the settlers from the Acadian region of Canada moved to French Louisiana, and some of their descendants later moved into

2

2) The Windmill Museum at Nederland is symbolic of the Dutch settlement that flourished here in the 19th Century. Some of the Dutch settlers' descendants still live in this area. 3) The Maison des Acadiens is a replica of a French Acadian home, characteristic of those built by descendants of the dispossessed French Canadians in Louisiana who settled in Texas.

southeast Texas. The Maison des Acadiens, adjacent to the Windmill Museum, is a replica of a typical French Acadian home. It is open Thursdays through Sundays from 2 to 6 p.m. from March through October, and 1 p.m. to 5 p.m. the rest of the year. Admission is free.

Port Arthur

Port Arthur is a thriving oil port and refinery center, but it did not get this way naturally. The original settlement here was founded in the 1840s, and it was known as Aurora. The water in Sabine Lake was not deep enough to make a port. Hurricanes were a problem. The settlers did a little fishing and farming, and most of them had moved somewhere else by 1890.

1) *Spindletop's oil boom spawned Port Arthur's development as a port city and the port is still an important factor in the movement of energy supplies.*

Then came an energetic railroad promoter named Arthur E. Stillwell. He was looking for a place where the trains on his Kansas City Southern Railroad could transfer cargoes to and from ocean-going ships. He decided that Port Arthur was that place. Stillwell bought some land and laid out a townsite and dredged a ship channel. Along the way, Stillwell lost control of his railroad empire to John W. Gates and ceased to be a factor. Gates was the famous speculator and financier known as Bet-A-Million Gates. He built a lavish home in the new city of Port Arthur. Only the foundation is standing today, but the home Gates' millionaire associate, Isaac Ellwood, built next door is one of the show places of Port Arthur.

Ellwood built a replica of a Pompeiian Villa. He had made a lot of money in barbed wire, and he went into partnership with John Gates in self-defense. He had so much trouble with Gates violating his barbed wire patents that he finally decided to make him a partner, and that is how Ellwood came into the Port Arthur picture. Ellwood's home was in Chicago. He thought the villa at Port Arthur would be a nice summer place, but he never got to live in it. He brought Mrs. Ellwood down from Chicago to see it shortly before it was finished. The mosquitoes were so bad that day, she decided the place was uninhabitable. She went back to Chicago without ever looking inside.

The villa is owned now by the city of Port Arthur. It is maintained by the Historical Society of Port Arthur. The address is

2) *Port Arthur's Bicentennial decoration program is still moving ahead as artists capture, on building exteriors, elements of the city's past cultures. 3) A fortune made in barbed wire helped early Port Arthur businessman Isaac Ellwood afford this elegant Pompeiian Villa. Mrs. Ellwood refused to live in it. Too many mosquitoes, she said.*

top era as can be found will be preserved. Gladys City is open to the public from 1 to 5 p.m., Sundays through Thursdays; and 9 a.m. to 5 p.m. on Saturdays. It is closed Fridays. There is a small admission fee.

The big oil discovery at Spindletop put Port Arthur in business as an oil port almost from the beginning. The population grew from 900 in 1900 to 10,000 in 1910.

Gulf and Texaco both operate big refineries in Port Arthur. Highway 87 passes through the Gulf Refinery and close by the tanker docks.

The people of Port Arthur decided in 1976 to decorate some of the buildings around town for the Bicentennial. They are trying to depict the history and the cultural heritage of their area in these paintings, and they didn't quit when the Bicentennial year ended. They are still painting. This mural about the Mexican contribution is on the thrift store at Proctor Street and Beaumont Avenue.

1) *A colorful Irish bartender from Houston, Dick Dowling, raised a company of 41 men and smashed the Union attempt to land at Sabine Pass in 1863. This memorial commemorates his upset victory. 2) A piece of machinery from a Union ship disabled by Dowling's artillery is on display outside Beaumont's port.*

Sabine and Sabine Pass

Sabine Pass was laid out in 1836 by Sam Houston and Philip Sublett. It was originally called Sabine City. Some rival developers established a town they called Sabine, a little closer to the mouth of Sabine Lake. Both towns were intended to become major ports, and Sabine was on its way to becoming a resort until a series of hurricanes in 1886, 1900 and 1915 almost wiped out both communities.

One of the important Texas encounters between Union and Confederate forces occurred here near the mouth of Sabine Lake in 1863. Union General William Franklin had sailed from New Orleans with 20 gunboats and 5,000 troops, intending to land at Sabine and capture Texas. The mouth of the Sabine was defended by Confederate Lieutenant Dick Dowling and 41 other Irishmen from Houston. Dowling had been a bartender in Houston. Most of his men had been dock workers. They had six cannons protected by some earthworks. They called it Fort Sabine or Fort Griffin. The first two gunboats that tried to get past the little fort

3) Crab fishermen usually have good luck in this channel between Port Arthur and Sabine. To fish for crab in Texas does not require a license.

were disabled by cannonfire. General Franklin abandoned them and took the rest of the fleet back to New Orleans. Dowling suffered no losses. He captured two federal gunboats and 315 prisoners, and he's been hailed as a hero ever since, especially on St. Patrick's Day. A statue of the hero of the Battle of Sabine Pass stands in a park dedicated to his memory, south of Sabine. The concrete bunkers here had nothing to do with Dowling. They were built to hold coast artillery shells during World War II. It's a nice spot for a picnic and a good place to view the ships enroute to and from Beaumont, Port Arthur and Orange.

A piece of machinery from one of the Union ships crippled by Dowling's cannon is on display outside the Port of Beaumont. It is a walking beam from the sidewheeler CLIFTON. (Tours of the port can be arranged through the guard at the gate.)

The channel between Port Arthur and Sabine is a popular fishing spot. FM 3322 runs alongside the channel almost to the beach. It does not give access to the beach. Crabbing is good in all the waterways around the Golden Triangle. Fishermen need a license. Crab fishermen do not.

The state carries on studies of the problems and habits of birds and marine life at the J. D. Murphree Wildlife Management Area in the marshes south of State Highway 73. Fishing and boating are permitted.

Eight miles west of Sabine Pass on State Highway 87 is the Sea Rim State Park. This park covers more than 15,000 acres and has more than five miles of frontage on the Gulf. It is a wintering area for migratory waterfowl. Some rare and endangered animals live here including the red wolf, the American alligator, the river otter and the muskrat. Fishing is permitted.

1) Airboats are used by state employees who supervise the work of the J. D. Murphree Wildlife Management Area. It is near 2) the Sea Rim State Park, which offers 15,000 acres of winter sanctuary for migrating waterfowl. Some rare and endangered mammals also live here.

There are provisions for overnight camping. This is a Class I Park. The entrance fee is $1.00 per car unless you have an annual permit. The entrance fee does not cover the use of camping shelters. There is an additional charge for shelters at this park and all the other state parks where shelters are provided.

State Highway 87 runs on southwest from here and connects at Port Bolivar with the Highway Department's free ferry to Galveston. The highway runs right beside the beach for more than 50 miles. The beach is wide open. Access is easy. You can pitch a tent or park your vehicle right beside the water. There are three fishing piers. In the other direction, Highway 87 crosses the Neches River on the spectacular Rainbow Bridge and leads to the port city of Orange, on the Sabine River.

. 3

4

3) This 1924 photo of the USS Patoka, with dirigible attached, explains why the Rainbow Bridge, near Orange (4) was built so high. Engineers wanted to be sure the tallest ships could get beneath it.

The Rainbow Bridge is the highest bridge in the South. It is higher than it needs to be. The Texas Highway Department started planning the bridge in the 1930s and wanted to make sure it would be high enough for any ship to pass under. The Department's engineers checked all around and found that the tallest ship afloat was the U. S. Navy dirigible tender PATOKA. The tender had a tall mooring mast for the Navy dirigibles AKRON and MACON. The Highway Department built the bridge higher than the PATOKA was tall. The bridge went into service in 1935. Both the AKRON and the MACON had crashed by that time and the PATOKA was no longer operating. But if a ship as tall as the PATOKA was ever needs to sail up the Neches waterway to Beaumont, it will have no trouble passing under the bridge on State Highway 87. The view is spectacular. But it is not a wide bridge and drivers better watch the other traffic instead of the view.

31

1) Orange County's present courthouse was built in 1936. Originally called Madison, the county changed its name in 1858, anticipating big orange crops that did not materialize.

ORANGE COUNTY

Orange County was originally a part of Jefferson County. It was established as a separate county in 1852. George Patillo selected the name because he thought his orange grove was going to turn out better than it did. The county seat was originally called Madison, but the name was changed to Orange in 1858. The present courthouse in Orange was built in 1936.

The Stark Art Museum on Green Avenue at 6th Street was built by the Nelda C. and H. J. Lutcher Stark Foundation in 1976. The Stark Foundation also restored the old W. H. Stark mansion as a cultural center.

The Farmers' Mercantile Company at Sixth and Division is a 1920s establishment still selling the same assortment of merchandise in the same atmosphere that prevailed when the place first opened.

Whatever Orange County lacks in orange production, it makes up in chemical production. Several big concerns have major plants here on what is known as Petrochemical Row, south of the port.

2

3

2) Nelda and H. J. Lutcher Stark, through a foundation, made possible the Stark Art Museum in Orange as well as restoration of the old mansion 3) directly across the street from the museum.

4) A holdover from the days when the "general store" was an American institution, the Farmers' Mercantile Company in Orange still sells merchandise of all kinds as it did in the 1920s.

1) This lumberjack, made of wood, standing before the court-house at Newton, makes it clear that this part of Texas is much concerned with timber. Early commerce in Newton County, from the 1880s, centered around the lumbering business and the county's huge stands of pine forecast a good future for that business.

NEWTON COUNTY

Above Orange County, between the Neches and Sabine is an area that was settled very early but never very densely.

Jasper and Newton counties are still mostly forest. These two counties originally were within the Spanish Municipality of Atascosito, but they had been established as the separate district of Bevil before the Revolution of 1836. The district was named for the original settler, John Bevil.

The government of the Republic established the district as Jasper County right after the Revolution.

Newton County was separated and established as a county in 1846. The man Newton County was named for never lived in the area. He was a hero of the U. S. Revolution named John Newton. Early settler John Bevil evidently was a history buff, and he had a hand in naming both these counties. (Jasper was named for U. S. Revolutionary War hero William Jasper.)

State Highway 87 runs north from Orange to the county seat of Newton County. The present courthouse at Newton has been in use since 1902. Across the street from the courthouse stands what is left of the W. H. Ford Male and Female College, founded in 1889. The wood cutout of the lumberjack on the courthouse grounds testifies that lumbering is the principal business in Newton County. The early settlers were farmers, but lumbering became the principal industry in the 1880s and it still is.

Newton County has some magnificent stands of pine, in the lowlands at the southern end of the county, and in the Blue Hills section in the north. The E. O. Siecke State Forest is on Farm Road 82, off State Highway 87 between Trout Creek and Bleakwood. There are provisions for camping here. Fishing and swim-

2) At a time when only a few pioneer families could afford to send children to college, W. H. Ford built this structure. The Ford Male and Female College, founded in 1889, has been preserved and restored as an educational landmark.

3

3) The E. O. Siecke State Forest in Newton County is a place where research continues into ways of growing bigger and better trees. It also affords the traveler a chance to hike nature trails, camp, fish and swim.

ming are permitted, and the forest service maintains a nature trail. Siecke Forest is named for a former State Forester.

There are not as many sawmills operating in Newton County today as there once were. But Weirgate, on Farm Road 1415, off State Highway 87, north of Newton, is one place that has a mill still working. The name Weir shows up in several places in Newton County because the Weir Lumber Company was one of the early operators here.

Sawmill workers mostly commute to work now. But in the early days, they lived in company towns alongside the mills.

1) This reconstruction of an early sawmill town at Newton is a far cry from how most sawmill workers live today. They are largely commuters who live in suburban homes. 2) Toledo Bend Reservoir is an increasingly popular public place for boating and fishing.

The people of Newton built a replica of an early sawmill town a few years ago, hoping it would become a tourist attraction. It seemed a good idea and it may yet succeed. But in the summer of 1977, Sawmill Town, U.S.A., was sadly displaying a sign offering the whole place for sale.

The southern end of the popular Toledo Bend Reservoir is at the northern end of Newton County. There is a public park alongside the dam. It is north and east of Burkeville where Farm Road 692 and 255 meet. There are public boat ramps. Swimming is permitted. There is a fee for camping.

JASPER COUNTY

U. S. Highway 190 links Newton with the county seat of Jasper County, to the west. The county courthouse at Jasper was built in 1889. The first settler in this county was John Bevil. He founded Bevilport on the Neches River, and he founded another settlement on Sandy Creek. The one on Sandy Creek was called Bevil until it was chosen to be the county seat, and then the name was changed to Jasper. Bevilport had been the commercial center of the area, but it went into a decline after the county seat was established at Jasper. Still standing is the home Randolph Doom built at Bevilport in 1852.

3

3) On many Texas courthouse squares, the outdoor domino game is a fixture of daily life. This one is at Jasper. 4) The Jasper County courthouse dates back to 1889. 5) One of the county's oldest surviving houses is the Randolph Doom home, built in 1852 and now owned by Congressman Jack Brooks.

4

5

1) *Most early Texas newspapers did not long survive the economics and rigors of frontier life. The weekly Jasper News Boy is an exception. It has been published here since 1865.*

2) *Jasper's Dixie Baptist Church is the successor to the church founded at this site in the 1850s by a slave on land given him by his owner. Like all Texas structures of historical significance, this one has the state 'medallion' affixed to a marker.*

The weekly *JASPER NEWS BOY* has been published here continuously since 1865.

The Dixie Baptist Church, west of Jasper, was founded in the 1850s by a slave named Richard Seale on land his master had given him. There is a state marker at the site of the church. The building standing here today is a newer one, but some of the people living in this area are descendants of the slaves who worked the land before the Civil War.

Jasper County's principal industries are sawmills and plywood plants. Kirbyville on U. S. 96, south of Jasper, was founded by lumberman John Henry Kirby in 1895.

3) *Zavala did not make it as a city. There once was a town here and a post office. The cemetery that survives is something of a mystery since the gravestones are not marked.*

Jasper County has some outstanding resorts for water sports. The lower end of the Sam Rayburn Reservoir is at the northern end of the county. The Twin Dikes Park beside the dam has campsites, trailer parking and docks.

The B. A. Steinhagen Lake is at the western edge of the county. The state maintains a park at the lake. This was once known as the "Dam B Park." It is now called the Martin Dies Jr. State Park. There is a camping area and shelters for rent. This is one of the state's Class I parks. There is a $1.00 entrance fee unless you have an annual permit. The annual permits can be obtained from the State Parks and Wildlife Department for $12.00. To reserve camp sites or shelters in this park, you can write Martin Dies Jr. State Park, Box 1108, Dogwood Station, Woodville 75979, or phone 713-384-5231. There are several other parks around Steinhagen Lake and most of them have provisions for camping and trailers.

One of the mysteries of Jasper County is the old cemetery at Zavala. There once was a settlement here and a post office. Nothing is left except the cemetery. The gravemarkers are the mystery. There are no names on them. But the old stones are arranged differently on each gravesite. It is believed the arrangements were intended to identify the people buried here, but nobody now knows how to interpret the arrangements.

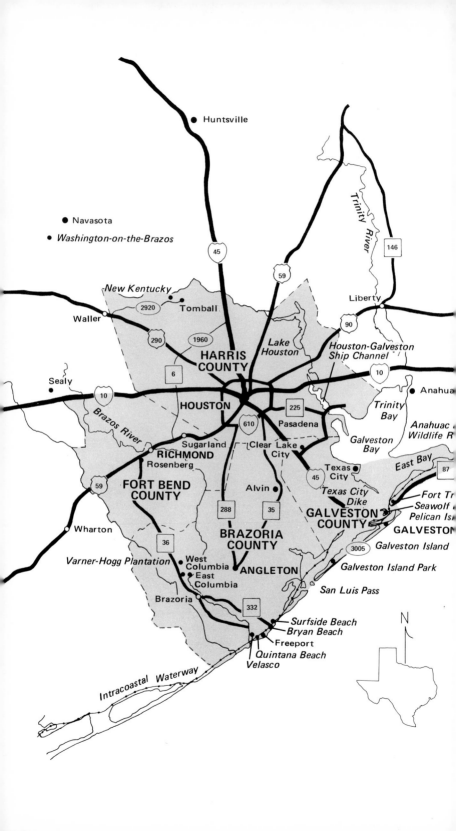

The Houston-Galveston Area

Galveston, Brazoria, Fort Bend and Harris counties

GALVESTON COUNTY

There are three ways to reach Galveston Island by motor vehicle. There is a toll bridge over San Luis Pass at the southwestern end of the island. There is a double causeway on Interstate 45 directly into the city of Galveston. But the most picturesque way to reach Galveston Island is by State Highway 87 from Port Arthur and Sabine Pass. There is no bridge, and the Highway 87 traffic is carried across the entrance to Galveston Bay on large ferryboats operated by the Texas Highway Department. This is also the slowest way because traffic waiting for the ferry often stacks up very deep.

Galveston County includes a big section of the mainland and half of Bolivar Peninsula in addition to the island.

The island probably was first discovered by Europeans in the early 1500s. Then, and for some time after that, the island was frequented by Karankawa Indians. Some accounts describe the Karankawas as cannibals. Some historians say that was a bad rap.

Little attention was paid to the island until pirates began using it as a base in the early 1800s. The most famous of the pirates operating from here was Jean Laffite. It's believed his headquarters were near where the University of Texas Medical complex is today. A state marker in the 1400 block of Water Street designates the spot where Laffite's house is believed to have stood. The foundations on the spot were part of a later building.

Several hundred people were living at Galveston by the time Texans declared their independence. Interim President David G. Burnet and his cabinet took refuge here during the Battle of San Jacinto, and this was where they learned their revolution had succeeded. Galveston became a city when M. B. Menard bought part of the island from the Republic and laid out the townsite. The city became the county seat when Galveston County was split off from Brazoria County in 1839.

41

1

2

1) Mammoth causeways span both Galveston Bay and the Intracoastal Waterway, linking Galveston Island with the nearby mainland. 2) Often called the "best free ocean trip in America," the Galveston-Bolivar Ferry hauls cars and people round trip across a picturesque stretch of bay and open water. There's no charge but waiting lines often are long. 3) Bernardo de Galvez, who never actually saw the island named for him, was a Spanish governor of Louisiana in 1777. He gave conspicuous aid to the colonists during the American revolution.

3

4

5

4) Because of its mild climate, Galveston attracts tourists to beaches like Stewart Beach Park from early spring to late fall and some hardy types in winter. There are about 30 miles of Galveston beach fronting the Gulf. 5) At one time this was the major port of Texas and while Houston now has that title, Galveston is still a major international shipping terminus.

The city and the county took their name from Galveston Bay. The bay had been named by an early Spanish surveyor. The surveyor was working for the Spanish governor, and he was just trying to please his boss by naming a nice bay for him. The governor was Bernardo de Galvez. He never laid his eyes on the bay or the island or the city.

The present Galveston County Courthouse is fairly new. It was built in the 1960s. . . . to replace a more ornate building that was damaged by Hurricane Carla.

1) *Galveston's historic "Old Red," is the Ashbel Smith building at the University of Texas Medical School. 2) Galveston County's courthouse is modern since earlier ones did not survive hurricanes. 3) The University of Texas Medical School is widely known as a teaching-treatment center.*

2

3

4) From late June through mid-October, Galveston residents are wary of storm clouds. That is the hurricane season and while modern advance warning techniques protect human life, everyone remembers 5) the fury and destruction of the famous 1900 Galveston hurricane. Such early storms prompted the city to erect its long, protective seawall.

5

The early settlers of Texas were a long time realizing what havoc the Gulf hurricanes could cause. Many promoters and settlers established towns and businesses right on the shore. The storms eventually persuaded the residents of many exposed communities, like Sabine and Indianola, that the low and sandy coast was too vulnerable.

But Galveston was established as the richest and most important city in Texas before it experienced its first great storm in 1900. There was too much to Galveston to be abandoned. After that storm swept over the island and killed 6,000 people, Galvestonians persuaded the federal government to put up a stout seawall to protect their island. Then they raised the level of the island behind that seawall, by pumping in silt and fill from the surrounding bays and channels. It was a prodigious effort, but it was either that, or abandon the island, or have the city wiped out periodically.

1) This is how an early Galveston photographer dramatized the height of the newly built seawall. 2) Construction of the seawall for the period was a major engineering feat. Builders had to compete with sand and tides as their project stretched out seven miles along the beach, fronting the Gulf of Mexico.

3) Galveston's surf is not comparable in size to the big waves off California and Hawaii, but it provides year-round recreation for thousands. Winters, generally, are mild and some water enthusiasts use wet suits to continue surfing even then, when the mean water temperature is about 60 degrees.

46

Two of Galveston's major beachfront hotel landmarks are (4) the venerable Galvez Hotel and (5) the newer Flagship Hotel. The latter is built on a large pier which extends out over the water.

The investment and effort paid off. Houston has since taken over Galveston's old status as the chief port and commercial center on the coast. But Galveston remains an important port and a major tourist center. The surf is not what you'd find in Hawaii or California, but there are plenty of surfers, anyway. The city has more than 30 miles of beaches on the Gulf. Accommodations range from campgrounds and mobile home parks to fine hotels.

The old Galvez on the Seawall is up-to-date and comfortable inside. The Flagship sits over the Gulf on a concrete pier built originally as an amusement park. Fishing is permitted from the end of the pier. The charge is $1.50 if you're not staying at the hotel.

Public fishing piers extend out into the Gulf, from 61st Street and from 91st Street. Prices are $1.50 at 61st Street and $2.00 at 91st Street. They are open all hours, all year.

The jetties at the entrance to the Galveston-Houston Ship Channel are very popular fishing spots, and free. Rollover Pass on Bolivar Peninsula is another popular free fishing spot.

1

Fishing is a major lure that draws thousands every week to Galveston waters. The zealous angler can fish 24 hours a day at such spots as 1) the Gulf Coast Fishing Pier, 2) Rollover Pass on the Bolivar Peninsula, 3) Galveston's wave-splashed "jetties." Specks and redfish are sought after by most fishermen here. Those who seek larger species go offshore in available charter boats.

2

3

Charter boats take fishermen on excursions into the bay and out into the Gulf. The charter boats dock at Pier 18. (The piers in Galveston line up, roughly, with the streets that have the same numbers.) Prices range from $6.00 for a few hours in the bay to $20.00 to $30.00 per person for a full day offshore.

Fresh fish, shrimp and oysters are available at Hill's and Fisherman's Wharf, near the charter boat docks. Both Hill's and Fisherman's Wharf have cooks on duty. You can buy fresh cooked fish, shrimp, crab or oysters and eat outdoors looking out over the shrimp boat basin, if you are not hopelessly addicted to air conditioning.

4) Those who prefer to buy their catch can do so along Galveston's wharves. Piers 19 and 21 in particular, are where fish markets offer a wide range of what fishing boats have brought in.

5) Waterfront dining is available at Hill's and at Fisherman's Wharf.

The Strand was the center of commerce when Galveston was the biggest and busiest city in Texas. A big fire wiped out some of the earliest buildings, a long time ago. But many of the buildings here today were built before the Civil War.

The Galveston Historical Foundation is leading a major effort to restore the old buildings on the Strand to usefulness. Several attractive shops and eating places have been established in the restored buildings on the Strand.

A Galveston County Historical Museum has been established in the former City National Bank Building at 2219 Market Street near the Strand. The Foundation has restored the old St. Joseph's Catholic Church at 2201 Avenue K, and it is open on Fridays during the summer months.

1) Galveston's shrimp fleet is part of a major Texas industry that operates
out of all coastal ports. Nearly 2,000 boats like these use a Y-shaped net
called a trawl to scour the relatively shallow inshore water, in search of
shrimp. This is the backbone of the commercial fishing industry of Texas.
2) First Presbyterian, at 1903 Church Street, is among the most imposing
old church buildings still in active use.

3) This was The Strand, at the peak of its commerce, in 19th Century Galveston. Galveston then was the largest and busiest of all Texas cities. Its port was the main entry point for the state, both for people and cargoes, and the wealth of the time could be seen in the fine business and residential buildings erected on or near The Strand. 4) Many of the old buildings and some of the original buildings still stand on the Strand. They are now being restored and preserved.

Galveston may have more 19th Century homes in good condition than any other city in the country. The prosperous people of this pleasant city built some sturdy houses. A great many of them have been preserved or restored as private homes, and they can only be viewed from the streets. But some are open to visitors. These include the one built by early settler Samuel May Williams in 1837 at 3601 Avenue P, the one Colonel Walter Gresham built in 1886-93 at 1402 Broadway (now known, usually, as the Bishop's Palace), and the one J. M. Brown built in 1859 at 24th and Broadway. This splendid old building served as Union Occupation Headquarters after the Civil War, and the order extending Lincoln's Emancipation Proclamation to Texas was reputedly issued from here. The building was the home of Galveston's El

51

1) Galveston's old City National Bank Building is now a museum, operated by Galveston County. It is near the Strand. 2) The Rosenberg Library, bequeathed by a successful early Galveston merchant, has become one of the most important repositories of historical, research and scholarly printed matter in Texas. It also continues as a public library, lending more than 100,000 volumes annually. Its collections of diaries, early manuscripts, rare books, early newspapers and Texas records are considered priceless and are much used by researchers and historians.

3) St. Mary's Cathedral, 2011 Church Street, was built at a time in Galveston's development when all denominations were erecting architecturally impressive buildings throughout the city. No town in the state had larger or finer churches in the late 19th and early 20th Centuries.

4

4) *The restored Post Office building on Postoffice Street in downtown Galveston is the oldest federal building in Texas. 5) The old Gresham home at 1402 Broadway has been called "The Bishop's Palace" since the Catholic Diocese owns it. The Bishop doesn't live here, and tours of the massive structure are available to the public. Its elegant, ornate architecture and interior appointments are considered classics of a period when homes were built as much for social recognition as for comfort.*

5

Mina Shrine for many years. There is a charge for admission at these three old homes and at St. Joseph's Church.

The tallest building on the island is the headquarters building of the American National Life Insurance Company. There is an observation deck on top, open to visitors during office hours on weekdays. The insurance company also maintains a small museum. The exhibits depict some of the history of the island and the company. American National carried the insurance on Bonnie and Clyde.

1

1) Galveston's historical foundation has restored this early building, St. Joseph's Church, 2201 Avenue K, to near mint condition. 2) Many of Galveston's tree-lined residential streets contain large old homes, built in the Victorian style, and survivors of the city's toughest hurricanes. 3) The Williams House, built in 1837 by early settler Samuel May Williams, is one of the city's earliest surviving homes. It is located at 3601 Avenue P.

2

3

4) *Ashton Villa was built by J. M. Brown in 1859 at 24th and Broadway. The building has had a long, interesting life. It was headquarters for Union forces which occupied Galveston briefly during the Civil War. Later, Galveston's El Mina Shrine made its home here. 5) From atop the American National Building can be seen part of Galveston's port panorama, including a portion of the city's 37 piers that can berth 100 vessels at once. At one time 69 steamship lines had offices in Galveston.*

1) Galveston's long seawall carries both a broad boulevard and spacious sidewalks and it affords the visitor opportunity for plenty of walking, cycling, or sightseeing from the tourist trains that are also available. Crowds are heaviest during the weekends in summer.

2) The Balinese Room, famous as a center for gambling in the years just prior to and after World War II, no longer offers games of chance; only dinners and theatre entertainment. Although sometimes damaged, it has managed to survive Gulf Coast hurricanes for four decades and remains one of the city's best-known landmarks.

The island has a tourist train. It boards passengers at Menard Park at Seawall and 27th and makes a trip around the city. The charge is $2.00 for adults and 75¢ for children, and free for children under four. The train runs every day in the summer and every day but Monday the rest of the year.

Gambling was never legal in Galveston, but it was widely tolerated in the 1930s and early 1940s. There were several well-known gambling resorts, and one of them is still highly visible. The Balinese Room offered fine food and entertainment, and there was plenty of action in the back rooms. They were crowded then with slot machines and crap tables, all designed to be disposed of

3

3) *The U.S. Army built this installation, Fort Travis, on Bolivar Point, across from Galveston Island. It contained heavy artillery pieces for coastal defense. Deserted now, it is being developed as a county park.*

4

4) *Fort Crockett's fine old homes for military personnel and a few surviving concrete blockhouses 5) are all that remain of a major U.S. Army installation that protected this section of the Gulf Coast in the long period from World War I through World War II. There were never any attacks during that period and the big gun emplacements near the beach, familiar to generations of tourists, are now nearly all gone.*

5

through the windows, into the Gulf, in case of a serious raid. The Balinese Room has been operated as a Supper Club and Dinner Theater in recent years. The gambling gear is gone, but the furnishings in the main dining room are substantially the same as were here in the days when you had to know somebody to get in.

There are military relics of several kinds around Galveston. The Republic established a fort at the eastern tip of the island and named it Fort Travis. The U. S. Army reestablished Fort Travis at Port Bolivar, on the opposite side of the channel. It was a coast artillery base. Somewhere near this spot, Mrs. Jane Long spent the winter of 1821 in a rude fort with only a small child

1

1) *Two retired U.S. Navy fighting ships, the World War II submarine Cavalla and the destroyer escort Stewart are on display at Seawolf Park on Pelican Island in Galveston Bay.*

and a servant girl. She was the wife of Dr. James Long. He was off in the interior of Texas trying to help the Mexicans win their independence from Spain. He was captured and killed. Jane Long later joined Stephen F. Austin's colony and made her own way as a boarding house operator and planter.

The Army built another fort on the Galveston side of the channel, about where the original Fort Travis had been and called it Fort San Jacinto. A third coastal artillery base was built on the beach. This one was called Fort Crockett. All three of these forts were manned through World War I and World War II, but there was never any action at any of them.

Fort Travis at Bolivar is being turned into a county park. It will eventually have overnight camping. Nothing much is left of Fort San Jacinto, but several of the Fort Crockett buildings are still standing and serving other purposes. The guns are all gone, but you can still see where some of them were on the Seawall between 48th and 53rd Streets.

The chief military event in Galveston's history occurred at the port. A Union naval force steamed in on Christmas Day in 1862 and seized a wharf and a warehouse. Confederate forces recap-

2

2) *Seawolf Park, popular for fishing as well as its old ships, includes a modern, enclosed pavil-
ion.* 3) *Just off the island is this
hulk — the remains of a 1922
experiment in building ships of
concrete. Named the Selma, its
hull cracked and the ship came to
rest in shallow water, a permanent
fixture of Galveston's harbor.*

tured the area on New Year's Day, a week later. Some Galveston
buildings were damaged in the exchange of cannon fire.

Galveston never was a naval base except briefly during the
days of the Republic, but two old U. S. Navy ships are on display
at Seawolf Park on Pelican Island, across the ship channel from
the port. The ships here are the World War II submarine
CAVALLA and the STEWART. The ships are open to visitors all
day every day. The charge is $1.00 for adults and 50¢ for chil-
dren. You can get to Pelican Island only one way. That is the
causeway on 51st Street. You turn east off Broadway.

Seawolf Park is situated on the site of the old Galveston Quar-
antine Station. All the immigrants to this country did not come
through Ellis Island. Thousands came directly to Texas and
landed at Galveston and cleared through the station the Immigra-
tion Service maintained here for many years.

Seawolf Park is another popular fishing spot. Off the island to
the northeast is the wreck of a World War I experimental concrete
ship, the SELMA. She was allowed to sink here in 1922 after she
was damaged in an accident, and she has been here ever since.
This is another popular fishing spot. Another one is the Texas

59

1

2

1) The Texas City Dike, made up of great boulders, runs five miles into Galveston Bay from the mainland near Texas City. It too is popular among fishermen. 2) Sea Arama Marine Park, on the Seawall, offers an outdoor marine show of mammals trained to do unusual tricks. There are several performances daily.

City Dike, extending five miles out into Galveston Bay from the great chemical and refining center on the mainland where they still hold memorial services every April 16th for the 461 people killed in the explosion that occurred on that date in 1947.

Sea Arama Marine Park is on Seawall Boulevard, on the island, at 91st Street. The park has a big aquarium and an outdoor marine show with performing mammals. There is a ski show and a children's petting zoo. Also on exhibit at Sea Arama is a sailing yacht from the 1930s. The schooner SOUTHWIND was owned by several movie celebrities including actor George Brent before Sea Arama acquired her in 1972. Admission prices at Sea Arama are $5.50 for adults and $4.50 for children under 12. Children under three are admitted free. Parking is $1.00 a car, but there is nothing to prevent you from parking on the boulevard if you can find space. The park is open every day of the year.

3

3) This sailing yacht, The South-wind, dates back to the 1930s, and is open to the public at Sea Arama. It once was sailed by movie stars of that earlier era.

4

5

4) Beyond the end of Galveston's seawall on FM 3005 is Galveston Island State Park. It is here that 5) "Lone Star," an historical drama, is staged during the summer.

Galveston Island State Park is about six miles beyond the end of the seawall, on Farm Road 3005. This was the old Maco Stewart Ranch until the state acquired it in 1970. There are provisions for day camping and also for overnight and extended camping. This is a Class I park. Entrance fee is $1.00 per car, unless you have an annual permit. An historical drama titled "Lone Star" is performed here in a handsome outdoor theater nightly except Mondays, during the summer months.

1) This type of waterfront home development has grown rapidly in recent years and the west end of Galveston Island is popular among second home owners as well as retirees. 2) The tollbridge across San Luis Pass connects west Galveston Island and Freeport. The current is swift here and the fishing action often brisk.

Several subdivisions have been developed on this end of the island with canals dredged in from West Bay, but there is a growing controversy over whether this kind of development should be allowed to continue in waters and marshes so important to marine life and waterfowl.

BRAZORIA COUNTY

Similar development is going on just as rapidly in Brazoria County, across the toll bridge at San Luis Pass. The bridge was built by Galveston County. The toll is supposed to be lifted when the bridge is paid for. Many saltwater fishermen call this pass their favorite fishing spot. There is a fishing pier in the Gulf on the Brazoria County side of the pass.

3

3) Relatively uncluttered with either improvements or people, Surfside Beach is part of the 20 miles of Brazoria County facing the Gulf. Roads parallel parts of the beach front and the Bryan Beach State Park offers camping and picnicking. 4) Only this marker remains to mark the location of an early Texan-Mexican battle -- The Battle of Velasco -- that was the forerunner of the 1836 war for Texas independence. Velasco was briefly the capital of the new Republic of Texas after the war was over.

4

Brazoria County has 20 miles of beach. Farm Road 3005 parallels the beach between San Luis Pass and Surfside. Nearby is the Bryan Beach State Park. Fishing, camping, swimming and picnicking are permitted, but no improvements have been built yet.

Brazoria County was one of the original Texas counties, formed from a Mexican municipality of the same name. The municipality was part of the original Stephen F. Austin colony.

The interim government of the Republic of Texas functioned briefly at old Velasco where Surfside is today. The first armed clash between Mexicans and Texans occurred here in 1832. The first President and first Congress of the Republic took office officially at Columbia (now West Columbia) in Brazoria County.

Angleton, county seat of historic Brazoria County, still has all the court-houses built since it became administrative center for the county. 1) This was the courthouse in the years from 1897 until 2) this newer courthouse was erected in 1940. The older building had a clock tower originally but it was blown down by a hurricane in the 1920s.

The original county seat of Brazoria County was Brazoria. It was moved to Angleton in 1897. The present Brazoria County courthouse in Angleton was built in 1940.

The Brazos River was the principal artery of commerce in the early days and up until the Civil War. The banks of the lower Brazos in Brazoria County were lined with plantations, where the owners and their families lived the kind of life Margaret Mitchell imagined in *Gone With the Wind*.

Steamboats like the YELLOWSTONE (built originally for the Missouri River trade) travelled up and down the river carrying passengers and cotton.

3) *This artist's sketch recalls one of the little Texas river steamers that played an important role in Texas history. The Yellowstone helped move the Texas army across the Brazos River, just prior to the climactic Battle of San Jacinto. It also ferried the victorious Texas government up and down Buffalo Bayou, as well as to Velasco.*

Several dams have been built on the Brazos since those days. The river fluctuated a great deal in depth before the dams were built, and it took the early settlers a few years to realize that the Brazos was not another Mississippi. Sometimes steamboats would go way up the river during a spring rise and get stranded and have to wait for another flood before they could steam back down again.

The spring of 1836 was a very wet spring. The Brazos had plenty of water in it. The YELLOWSTONE was up at Groce's Plantation near San Felipe when Sam Houston was moving his little army eastward to avoid Santa Anna's Mexican forces. Houston commandeered the YELLOWSTONE to move his men across the Brazos. That was March 31st, just three weeks before Houston and Santa Anna would meet at San Jacinto. The YELLOWSTONE played a further role in Texas history when she carried the interim government of the Republic from Galveston up to San Jacinto after the battle and then carried the government and Houston and Santa Anna from San Jacinto to old Velasco. Here, where Surfside is today, Santa Anna was obliged to sign the treaty that set Texas free.

Velasco and Quintana, on the other side of the mouth of the Brazos, were important resorts and ports before the Civil War. Galveston siphoned off most of the business after the first intracoastal waterway was built from the Brazos to Galveston Bay. Hurricanes eventually did in the resorts, and finally the mouth of the river itself was moved to accommodate the port of Freeport.

Freeport, which grew up on the water, is a city of boats as well as manufacturing. 1) Its shrimp fleet is one of the most active along the Gulf Coast. 2) Charter boats for offshore fishing are kept busy by growing interest in the larger, deepwater species. 3) Facilities for ocean-going vessels in recent years have made Freeport a major shipping terminus.

Freeport is now the principal seaport and the biggest city in Brazoria County. It is the home of the vast Dow Chemical Company Texas complex and the principal partner in the Brazosport trade and development system.

Shrimping is big business here, too. And there is a charterboat fleet based here running expeditions into the Gulf.

4

4) When the new Republic of Texas set up shop after its 1836 victory, it selected Columbia for its first legislative headquarters. This replica shows the kind of small buildings that housed the Texas House and Senate. Members of the first Texas Congress voted here to move their capital to Houston where they expected to be more comfortable. This area is now part of West Columbia.

The present towns of East Columbia and West Columbia, up the Brazos from Freeport, both developed out of an early plantation settled by Josiah Bell. West Columbia was originally called Columbia. It had a population of about 3,000 that summer of 1836 when the new government of the Republic of Texas was looking for a place to settle. There was a hotel, and some of the homes had extra rooms, so it was to Columbia that Sam Houston and the members of the first Congress came to take their oaths and begin their work. The House and Senate met in separate, small buildings. They are both gone now, but a replica of one of them has been built here. The members of the first Congress voted here in December of 1836 to move the capital to Houston where they were assured they would be more comfortable.

The first colonist of Texas was named Secretary of State in the first Houston cabinet. That was Stephen F. Austin, but he never lived to see the first anniversary of the colonists' victory. Austin died in December of 1836, and he was buried originally at his sister's plantation in Brazoria County. Austin's sister was Mrs. James F. Perry. She and her husband established their Peach Point Plantation in 1832. Austin helped design it and plan it, and he considered it his home, too. Part of the plantation is still in the Perry family, and descendants of Mrs. Perry still live here. But Peach Point is not open to the public.

The plantation home of former Governor James Hogg is open to the public. It is a state park. It is known as the Varner-Hogg Plantation State Park. It is on Farm Road 2852, two miles northwest of West Columbia. The plantation was established by one of Austin's original colonists named Martin Varner. Hogg acquired the property later, and his daughter, Ima, restored the place and presented it to the state in 1956.

1) Peach Point Plantation was built by James F. Perry and his wife in 1832. Mrs. Perry was the sister of Stephen F. Austin. He helped the Perrys design it and lived there for a time himself. The plantation is still in the Perry family. 2) Bailey's Prairie is a ghostly area, heavily hung with Spanish moss. It was settled by James Brit Bailey in 1821 and his ghost is still supposed to haunt the neighborhood.

3) This is the restored home of former Governor James Hogg, and is called the Varner-Hogg Plantation State Park. It originally was built by an early colonist named Martin Varner. Miss Ima Hogg restored the place and presented it to the State.

Two of the major crops in Brazoria County are 4) cotton and 5) rice. Its location in the coastal plain prompted early settlers to come there primarily to farm the cheap, rich land and raise livestock on plentiful grasses.

Some people claim to believe that the ghost of one of Austin's original colonists haunts the area around Bailey's Prairie. James Brit Bailey settled here in 1821. He was a fearless man, regarded as honest, upright and eccentric. He proved his eccentricity by insisting before he died in 1833 that he be buried in an upright position. He was buried that way, and there have been reports from time to time ever since that old Brit Bailey's ghost was seen here or there around Bailey's Prairie. There is enough Spanish moss on the trees around here to give the place a ghostly aspect.

The State Department of Corrections operates four large prison farms in the Brazos Valley in Brazoria County for the same reason the planters settled here. Conditions for growing crops are about as good here as they get anywhere. The prison farms were private plantations before the state acquired them.

1) The old Imperial Sugar Cane plant in Fort Bend County still processes sugar cane, but it is largely imported. In earlier times when the plant was built the area had many sugar cane plantations. None is left today. Fort Bend, and Brazoria County, were among the richest areas of Texas, and prior to the Civil War many of the largest 19th Century Texas fortunes had been made here.

FORT BEND COUNTY

Farming was the principal business in Texas in the years before the Civil War, and Brazoria and Fort Bend counties were among the most prosperous areas in the state.

Country club subdivisions may cover up Fort Bend County if developments continue at the present rate. But Fort Bend is still mostly farms and ranches. There were sugar plantations here in the early days. None of those is left, but the old Imperial Sugar Plant is still busy in Sugarland, processing imported sugar cane.

This county also was part of the original Stephen F. Austin colony. It was split off from Austin County and established as a separate county in 1837.

The population is concentrated in the twin cities of Richmond and Rosenberg. Richmond is older. Rosenberg is bigger, and it is also one of the few cities of its size to be served by two passenger trains. The Amtrak trains running between New Orleans and California and between Houston and Chicago both stop at the modest station in Rosenberg.

Rosenberg was established when the Santa Fe tracks were laid through here. It was named for Henry Rosenberg of Galveston. He was one of the railroad backers.

Richmond apparently was named for the capital of Virginia because a number of the early settlers here came from there. The city was built on the site of the early building that gave Fort Bend County its name.

2) Here is where the settlement of Fort Bend began in 1821. There never really was a fort at this bend in the Brazos River but the big log house built by early settlers looked sturdy enough to be called a fort. So they began calling the settlement, and later the county, Fort Bend. 3) What remains of north-south and east-west railroad service through Texas still runs through Rosenberg. Passengers can use this little station to go to New Orleans, California or Chicago by Amtrak. Rosenberg actually became a town when the Santa Fe tracks were laid through this area during the early day railroad-building era.

3

The Brazos River makes a bend around the present city. The first settlers built a stout log house here on the high west bank of the bend. The bend is a most emphatic bend. The log house never was really a fort. But the settlers called it one, and they eventually began calling it Fort Bend. When they needed a name for their county, they picked Fort Bend. The site where the fort stood is just north of the eastbound bridge on U. S. 59, on the Richmond side of the river.

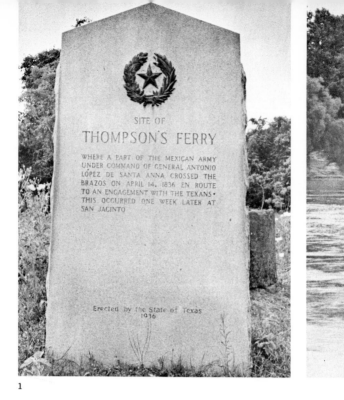

1

An early settler named Jess Thompson established a ferry service across the Brazos in about 1828 a short distance north of the old fort. The site was selected because the bottom and the banks are more rocky and less sandy here than most places on the Brazos. Thompson was killed in a gunfight before his ferry boat got involved in the war between the Mexicans and the Texans.

Santa Anna's army made a stop here in April of 1836 on the way to San Jacinto. Santa Anna was convinced by this time that the war was over. Sam Houston seemed to be on the run. The Anglo colonists were fleeing for the Louisiana border. The settlers at Fort Bend had left their homes and most of their belongings and crossed to the east bank of the Brazos. They scuttled the ferryboat.

The Mexicans found the ferryboat and salvaged it. Most of the Mexican troops stayed here and looted and burned the settlement while Santa Anna took a small force of crack troops on eastward to try to capute the rebels' interim government at Harrisburg. Mexican accounts say the generals Santa Anna left in charge of the force at Thompson's had a time trying to decide whether they should try to rescue him after he was captured by Sam Houston at San Jacinto. They probably had the force to do it. But they decided to return to Mexico.

The steamboat YELLOWSTONE passed by Thompson's on its way back from carrying Houston's army across the river at

1) It was here that in 1828 Jess Thompson established a ferry across the Brazos River. 2) There is little to see now but the site was important to how the Battle of San Jacinto turned out. Santa Anna left much of his army here to loot and burn while he marched off looking for Sam Houston's Army. He found it — and defeat.

Groce's place. The Mexican soldiers still camped here tried to lasso the steamer's smokestacks from the riverbank. They missed.

This ought to be a good place for some scrupulous digging. But it is on private property. The only readily apparent objects are the state marker and a couple of old cisterns probably built by Dr. George Feris. He had a horse farm here from the early 1840s until sometime in the 1890s.

Richmond has been the county seat of Fort Bend County from the beginning. The present courthouse was built in 1908. An earlier courthouse about two blocks north of the present one was the scene of a wild gun battle in 1889. It was called the Jaybird-Woodpecker War. The Woodpeckers were public officials elected and supported by the blacks during Reconstruction. The Jaybirds were the old line politicians supported by the wealthy residents and most of the white voters. The Jaybirds made a big effort to regain control of the county offices in the election of 1888. They failed, and there were some random killings over the next few months climaxing in a shootout around the courthouse August 16, 1889. It would be hard to say who won the battle, but the Jaybirds won the war. The Texas Rangers and the Nation-

1) The Fort Bend County Courthouse at Richmond is a peaceful scene today. It was not so peaceful in 1889 when 2) an earlier courthouse was in business. 3) This Jaybird monument marks the spot where a spectacular gunbattle erupted to decide which political faction ran the county. The Jaybirds won and put up the marker.

al Guard and the Governor came in and mediated. The upshot was a reorganization that put the Woodpeckers out and the Jaybirds in.

Richmond was the home of Mirabeau B. Lamar. He was the second president of the Republic and a hero of San Jacinto. He is

4

6

4) There isn't much left of Jane Long's famous early boarding house at Richmond except this old photo and a marker at the site. Both the graves of 5) Mirabeau B. Lamar and 6) Jane Long are well tended in the old Morton Cemetery on Second Street.

buried here in the old Morton Cemetery on Second Street, north of the business district. This cemetery dates back to colonial days. It is very well kept. Jane Long is buried here. She was called the "Mother of Texas" because she was supposed to have been the first Anglo woman to come to Texas. She lived in Richmond a long time, and for part of that time she kept a boarding house on 4th Street. The place was frequented by the most prominent politicians of the Republic. Several of them proposed to her. There are some steps and a marker at the site.

*Restaurants may survive where old homes do not. These two historic struc-
tures in Richmond are newly converted to eating places: 1) The General
Mercantile store on Morton Street and 2) The Colonel P. E. Peareson home
on 9th Street.*

Carrie Nation had a hotel in Richmond before she started
destroying saloons. She was here in the early 1880s.

A couple of the older buildings in Richmond have recently
been converted into restaurants.

The Fort Bend County Museum on Houston Avenue at 5th
Street has some interesting exhibits. It is open 9 a.m. to 5 p.m.
Tuesday through Saturday, and 1 p.m. to 5 p.m. Sundays. Sam
Houston's noted scout, Deaf Smith, died at the home of a friend
here in 1837, and it is believed he is buried on the museum
grounds. A recent addition to the museum is the old mansion
built by Congressman John M. Moore at 406 Fifth Street.

Descendants of Austin colonist Henry Jones are establishing a
park around the old Jones family cemetery on Farm Road 762,
south of Richmond. Some historic old homes from around the
Richmond area are being moved to the site to be restored and
preserved.

3) Deaf Smith's passing is marked by this Richmond marker. He was Sam Houston's famous scout who may have been hard of hearing but had no trouble understanding and carrying out Houston's order to burn the bridge that cut off any possibility of retreat from the San Jacinto battleground. He lived 18 months after the Texas Revolution was won.

4

5

4) Preservation of early homes has become a major industry in Fort Bend County. This is the mansion of Congressman John M. Moore, now a museum on Fifth Street. 5) The Henry Jones family cemetery and some old homes are being restored in a park south of Richmond.

1) *Houston, seen from a nearby park, presents a constantly changing skyline, so great has been its growth in recent years. Now the nation's fifth largest city, it grew out of a swampy, mosquito-infested village that began as the Texas Revolution ended in 1836. For a time it was the new Republic's capital. 2) This was the capitol building on Texas Avenue where 3) the Rice Hotel stands today. Houston's early growth resulted in part from its location on Buffalo Bayou, which meandered to the Gulf. Construction of the Houston Ship Channel in 1914, giving the port access to world shipping, made Houston one of the nation's major seaports.*

HARRIS COUNTY

Harris County was another one of the original counties established by the government of the Republic in 1836. The name of
the county was Harrisburg until 1839 when it was shortened to
Harris. The area had previously been the Municipality of Harrisburg, and the town of Harrisburg was the principal settlement.
Santa Anna burned Harrisburg.

A couple of New York land speculators named John and
Augustus Allen founded the City of Houston a little farther up
Buffalo Bayou before Harrisburg could be rebuilt. Houston was
designated the county seat, and the Allen brothers persuaded the
government of the Republic to move the capital of Texas from
Columbia to Houston by promising to build and donate a capitol
building. The Capitol stood on Texas Avenue where the Rice
Hotel is today until the government decided to move to Austin in
1839.

The location of the capitol here gave Houston some momentum, but the loss of the capitol had little effect. The momentum
was going then, and it has been going ever since. It infects the
residents.

You may see signs announcing that the speed limit is 55 m.p.h.
or less, but do not dawdle on Houston freeways or the 610 Loop.
The commuters will run over you.

Shallow draft boats could come up Buffalo Bayou to Houston
from the start. They don't anymore — but the original landing is
now a city park. It is alongside the Main Street Viaduct.

Improvements to the Buffalo Bayou channel began almost
immediately. The federal government was persuaded to join in
development of the Houston Ship Channel in 1914, and the chan-

1) Allen's Landing, where Buffalo Bayou goes through downtown Houston, was where early water-borne traffic deposited freight and passengers, as shown in this early photo. Today 2) the area has been made into a municipal park. There is virtually no boat traffic on the bayou today since all the ships that come up the ship channel stop in the port turning basin. A bayou beautification program, began years ago, has helped make a part of the waterway attractive, and some parts of it are used for small paddle boat races.

nel has made Houston one of the principal seaports in the United States. The wharves and warehouses are arranged mostly around the upper end of the channel that begins at the mouth of Galveston Bay. The visitors' entrance to the Port of Houston is off Clinton Drive. There is an observation deck. And there is an inspection boat called the SAM HOUSTON. This is a comfortable yacht with air conditioning, and visitors can arrange to ride it. But the arrangements have to be made well in advance with the Houston Chamber of Commerce.

3

4

5

3) The long lens camera shows Houston's skyline rising in the distance beyond the port's turning basin. Houston's role as world energy headquarters and its growing status as an agricultural and chemical shipping terminus has meant that its port 4) is crowded with the traffic of many nations. 5) The Sam Houston takes visitors on tours of the Houston Ship Channel.

1) Few buildings showing in the Houston skyline are more than one or two decades old, so quickly have newer buildings replaced older ones. It was fortunate that the early municipal planners provided for wide streets in the central business district, in view of the volumes of traffic that modern freeways deposit into downtown Houston each day. Many of the large buildings are also linked by underground and over-the-street pedestrian walkways.

Houston is growing so fast that some of the early landmarks have been torn down to make way for new buildings that have since been torn down to make way for newer ones. The process can be observed almost anywhere in the downtown area and around the loop system.

A few old buildings in the area around the site of the original City Hall have been preserved. This is the area called Market Square because the grounds around the City Hall were a produce market in the early days. The site is now a park, and the city government operates in a building put up by the WPA on Bagby Street, in the 1930s.

The original Houston Cotton Exchange Building is one of the old buildings that has been preserved and restored. It is at the corner of Travis and Franklin. This building was built in 1884, and the Houston Cotton Exchange operated here until it moved to a new building in the 1920s.

The present Harris County Courthouse at Fannin and Congress was built in 1884. The county government has outgrown the building and has built three courthouse annexes on property surrounding the old courthouse.

2

2) The original Houston Cotton Exchange Building is an early downtown landmark. 3) The Houston City Hall is part of a municipal center that includes a new library building, Sam Houston Coliseum and Music Hall, and City Hall Annex. 4) Old Market Square, now a park, is where the city's produce merchants once operated. 5) Harris County's old civil courts building stands beside several modern annexes in the downtown district.

3

5

1) The growing effort to preserve historic homes started in time to save some of the most beautiful, and in some cases serviceable, old mansions in Houston. This former home of oilman T. P. Lee is now the University of St. Thomas administrative building. 2) The Rice-Cherry house in Sam Houston Park once was the home of Rice University founder William Marsh Rice.

Many fine old homes have been demolished to make way for commercial expansion in Houston. But a few have survived. The University of St. Thomas on Montrose has its offices in the former home of oilman T. P. Lee, and the school conducts some of its classes in the home where Howard Hughes lived as a boy. There has been some restoration of old homes in the Montrose area around St. Thomas and also in the Houston Heights area along Heights Boulevard north of Washington Avenue.

Several of the city's historic buildings have been moved to the Sam Houston Park just west of the City Hall. This site was a plantation in the 1840s. Nathaniel Kellum owned the place, and he built a brick home he later sold to Abram Noble. The city bought the house and 20 acres of land in 1895. This was Houston's first city park. The Parks Department used the old plantation house as a warehouse and tool shed until the late 1950s when the Harris County Heritage Society persuaded the city to let it take responsibility for restoring the Kellum-Noble House. The Society later moved other old buildings here and restored them, and they are open for tours every day. There is a fee.

3

3) The Kellum-Noble House, built on this site in 1847, was erected by Houston's first brick manufacturer and represents a blend of Greek Revival and southern plantation architecture. 4) Courtland Place, in the Montrose district, has some elegant examples of Victorian design. 5) Sam Houston Park, in the shadow of the downtown business district, now contains a collection of Houston's restored, historic homes dating from the frontier period to the Victorian era.

4

5

Here are other buildings that have been restored in Sam Houston Park and are open for public tours. 1) This early Harris County farm house shows the rough-hewn timbers and logs that were used to fashion an early settler's home. There was no single style for building such a home. Early Texans, coming from all over the U.S. and Europe usually built the kind of homes they were accustomed to wherever they came from. 2) One of the city's earliest churches is also a fixture of Sam Houston Park's historic area. It is a five minute walk from the downtown skyscrapers.

One of the finest homes in the expensive River Oaks section of Houston is open to visitors. This is Bayou Bend. It was built and occupied for many years by the late Ima Hogg. She filled the house with rare antiques and turned the grounds into a park and then presented the place to the Houston Museum of Fine Arts. The house fronts on Lazy Lane in River Oaks, but the visitors' entrance is off Memorial Drive at Westcott Street. The Bayou Bend tour schedule is so complicated it would be best to call, 713-529-8773.

Houston has no high level observation points except for private clubs and restaurants. Most visitors will not be able to get into the private clubs. The public restaurants with views of the city are the Spindletop Room at the Hyatt Regency, 1200 Louisi-

3

3) The Spindletop Room atop the Hyatt Regency Hotel, at center of photo, is one of the unusual downtown eating places where patrons get an excellent view of the city. It slowly revolves. 4) Bayou Bend in River Oaks was the Ima Hogg mansion in River Oaks. Its grounds are opened periodically to the public so that people can enjoy its gardens and flowers.

4

5

5) Few people have had such an impact on a city's cultural life as Miss Ima Hogg did on that of Houston. The daughter of former Governor James Hogg, Miss Ima, as she was called, used much of the family's fortune for philanthropic purposes. She restored old homes for public use, collected antiques and other art objects so that her own home could ultimately become a part of the Houston Museum of Fine Arts. She became, in her long life, virtually a one-person movement for cultural improvement.

1

2

1) *Interiors of Bayou Bend, the Hogg home in Houston's River Oaks, show the magnificence that successful early Texas families sought to bring to their homes. Large sums of money were spent by the timber, railroad and early oil magnates to import from all over the world the finest examples of period furniture and appointments. 2) The antiques and architecture visible in the Hogg mansion draw crowds of visitors each year to see this carefully preserved example of gracious living from the early 20th Century. 3) The Annunciation Church, at Texas and Crawford streets, has been a highly visible place of downtown Houston worship for more than half a century.*

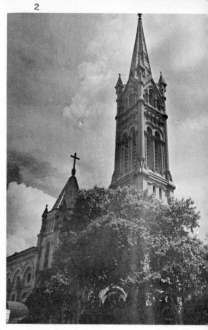

3

ana, downtown; Cody's in the Montrose Place Building, at Montrose and Hawthorne; and the Galleria Roof, in the Houston Oaks Hotel, at Westheimer and Post Oak.

There once were several churches in downtown Houston. Most of them have followed the population to the suburbs. Among those left in the inner city are the old Annunciation Catholic Church across Texas Avenue from the Union Station, Christ Church Episcopal Cathedral at 1117 Texas, and Antioch Baptist Church at 313 Robin. Antioch Baptist was founded by freed slaves more than a hundred years ago. It is surrounded now by expensive commercial buildings, and the members have been offered very big prices for the land their church stands on. They have rejected all the offers so far.

Grayline Tours offers sightseeing trips by bus. The ticket

5

Two other historic churches near the downtown area now surrounded by mushrooming business construction are 4) Christ Church Cathedral at the busy Texas and Fannin intersection, and 5) Antioch Baptist Church at 313 Robin. Because they were in the path of commercial development, many other large, old downtown church buildings have been demolished.

office has moved several times, though. Better check the phone book.

Visitors to Houston usually want at least to drive by the Astrodome. You can drive by free. Tours of the dome cost $2.00 plus $1.00 for parking. Admission to the Astroworld Amusement Park is $7.95 per person plus parking. The park is open every day from 10 a.m. to midnight in the summer, and on weekends in the spring and fall. It is closed during the winter months.

The Astrodome and Astroworld are on the 610 Loop South. If you are driving there out Main Street from downtown, you will pass the Rice University Campus on your right. If you are driving from downtown out Fannin Street, you will pass Hermann Park and Zoo and then the Texas Medical Center where Dr. DeBakey and Dr. Cooley work, on your left.

The coastal plain where the armies commanded by Santa Anna and Sam Houston finally fought April 21, 1836, is now the San Jacinto State Park. Buffalo Bayou has become the Houston Ship Channel. The old battleship TEXAS is parked at the edge of the battleground. It is open to visitors every day. There is an admission fee of $1.00 for adults, 50¢ for children between six and 11, and children under six are admitted free.

Places on the battleground where significant actions occurred are marked, and there is a museum in the base of the monument. The museum is open every day during the summer and every day except Sunday the rest of the year. The monument is nearly 600 feet tall. There is an observation platform at the top, and visitors

1) Sometimes called the Eighth Wonder of the World, the Astrodome, together with its nearby 2) Astroworld amusement park, constitute one of Houston's chief claims to entertainment fame. The Astrodome, when it was built, was the nation's first covered, air-conditioned baseball and foot-ball stadium. It attracted worldwide attention because of its engineering and bold concept, and it has proved its practicality over the years. Nearly 50,000 people can watch a baseball game here, out of the weather. Many visitors go through the Astrodome on tours, simply to see its cavernous interior.

3) The Texas Medical Center is a vast collection of teaching, diagnostic and treatment hospitals near the intersection of Houston's South Main Street and Holcombe Boulevard. Physicians and other hospitals throughout the world send patients here for highly specialized types of treatment, especially those relating to cancer and heart problems. Nearly two dozen hospital buildings make up the complex. 4) Nearby is the long stretch of greenery, lakes and zoo that make up Hermann Park. This statue at the entrance depicts Sam Houston, it is said, pointing toward San Jacinto's battleground.

4

5

5) Rice University, across South Main from the Texas Medical Center, has long been one of Houston's major educational landmarks. It opened for instruction in 1912 and was endowed from the estate of its founder, William Marsh Rice. The University — formerly called Rice Institute — spreads across 300 acres and is noted particularly for its engineering, architecture and science instruction. It was not until 1965 that the University began to charge tuition. Expansion programs in the past two decades have made it possible for many more students to attend Rice than in its earlier years.

1) The San Jacinto Battleground, now a state park, commemorates the spectacular victory that won Texas independence on April 21, 1836. Cannon and markers spread around the grounds tell what sort of engagements took place on that day. 2) The old Battleship Texas, retired after World War II, has been preserved in a slip adjacent to the battlefield and is open to the public. It fought in both world wars. The battlefield proper is about 45 minutes from downtown Houston.

4

3) This tall spire marks the site where Sam Houston's main force of 910 Texans assaulted Santa Anna's army of more than 1,300 on the afternoon of the battle. The Texans started from where the trees stand 4) at the edge of the bayou and advanced up the slope where the lagoon is now. It was one of the most important and lopsided battles in history. The Texans killed 630 of the enemy and took 730 prisoners, including Santa Anna, losing but nine men themselves. As a result of this action, nearly one-third of the continent — most of the West — later became part of the United States.

can get there by elevator during periods when the museum is open.

The battleground has been sinking along with most of the other land around Galveston Bay. The owners of the old San Jacinto Inn have built a new establishment, duplicating the old one, on higher ground because water got so high around the old one sometimes the customers had to enter and leave by boat.

1) *An echo of the past, the Lynchberg Ferry is still operating near the San Jacinto Battleground. Nathaniel Lynch operated a ferry here as early as 1836 and there's been one here as long as anybody can remember. Today's ferry is operated by the county and it's free.*

The Texas scout, Deaf Smith, destroyed the wooden bridge over Vince's Bayou before the Battle of San Jacinto started. The Bayou was flooded, and the destruction of the bridge cut off any chance that the Mexicans or Texans either could escape quickly from the battleground area. The site of Vince's bridge is in the present city of Pasadena on Richey Street right off State Highway 225.

A ferry boat still operates between the battleground and the settlement of Lynchburg where Nathaniel Lynch was operating Lynch's Ferry in 1836. There were some complaints about the fares Lynch charged in the old days, but Harris County operates the Lynchburg Ferry today, and it is free.

Another place that figured in the events leading up to the Texas victory at San Jacinto was the town of New Kentucky. It was at the spot where the old Atascosito Road and the colonists' road between Washington-on-the-Brazos and Harrisburg crossed. Houston had been moving his army eastward. Santa Anna and many Texans thought Houston was headed for the safety of the Louisiana border. At New Kentucky, Houston took the road south toward Harrisburg and San Jacinto and made it plain that he meant to fight. It was an important decision and New Kentucky was an important settlement at that time. But it did not survive. The site is now a Harris County Park. It is on the Waller-Tomball Road, about nine miles west of Tomball. Some of the history of the settlement at New Kentucky is preserved in the Magdalene Charlton Memorial Museum in Tomball.

2

2) The Lyndon B. Johnson Manned Spacecraft Center at Clear Lake, south of Houston, has been the point from which America's spacecraft and astronauts have been guided on their flights. This is the project management building, called Building One, and is part of the large complex where astronauts are trained and near which most of them live.

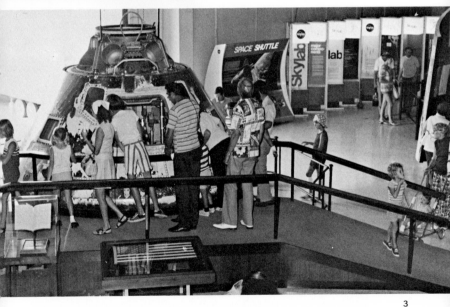

3

3) As American spacecraft began leaving and returning to earth in increasing numbers, the size of the exhibits and space required for them has continued to grow at NASA headquarters near Houston. Regular tours and film lectures are provided for the public and the center is open to visitors each day. On display are some of the space capsules used by the early astronauts, showing how cramped were their quarters compared to the current space shuttle flights that have commenced.

The Lyndon B. Johnson Manned Spaceflight Center is in southern Harris County on a road specially designated NASA Road 1. No manned spaceflights ever took off from here, but most of them were managed and controlled from here. Some of the early rockets and space capsules are on exhibit. The Space Center is open to visitors 9 a.m. to 4 p.m. every day. The spectacular trips to the moon are history now. But the NASA people are busy with plans for flights in space ships that can return to earth and fly again, and they are sure to play the major role in development of the space solar energy stations we are going to have to have eventually.

Other museums in the Houston area:
Contemporary Arts Museum
5216 Montrose
Open weekdays and Sunday afternoons. Free.

Museum of Fine Arts
1001 Bissonnet at Main
Open daily except Mondays. Free.

Museum of Natural Science and Planetarium
5800 Caroline
Open every day. Free.

Museum of Medical Science
5800 Caroline
Open every day. Free.

Baytown Historical Museum
2407 Market Street, Baytown
Open Mondays through Fridays. Free.

Pasadena Historical Museum
Highway 225 at Memorial Park, Pasadena
Open daily during summer months. Free.

Principal shopping centers:

Almeda Mall
I-45 South at Almeda-Genoa Road, Southeast Side

Galleria
5015 Westheimer at Post Oak, West Side

Greenspoint Mall
I-45 North at North Belt, near the airport

Gulfgate Mall
I-45 South at the 610 Loop, Southeast Side

Northwest Mall
610 Loop at Highway 290, West Side

Memorial City Mall
I-10 West at West Belt, West Side

Sharpstown Mall
U. S. 59 South at Bellaire Boulevard, Southwest Side

Westbury Square
West Bellfort at Chimney Rock, Southwest Side

Westwood Mall
U. S. 59 South at Bissonnet, Southwest Side

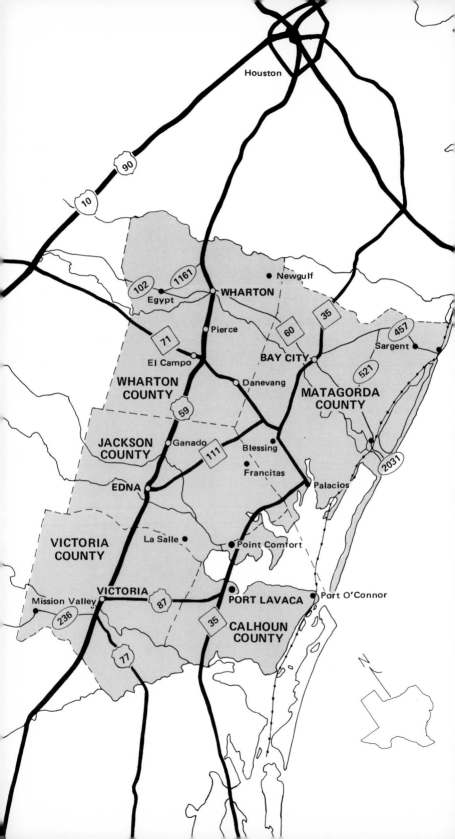

The Middle Coast

Wharton, Victoria, Jackson, Calhoun
and Matagorda counties

Some of the land on the middle coast of Texas was included in Stephen F. Austin's colony. Plantations and farms flourished here before the Civil War. The earliest explorers passed this way. LaSalle got stranded here with a couple of hundred French colonists, but they never made it French. It is not even certain they ever wanted to.

This is rice and cattle country, with substantial oil production and a very large sulphur deposit.

WHARTON COUNTY

U. S. Highway 59 runs right through the middle of Wharton County, and it will take you around the city of Wharton or through it. It is your choice.

Wharton County was formed in 1846 from parts of Matagorda and Jackson counties. The city of Wharton has been the county seat from the beginning. Twenty-five of Stephen F. Austin's original 300 colonists got their land grants in this vicinity.

The county and the county seat were named for two brothers. John and William Wharton settled here in the 1830s. They were both lawyers and both among the early agitators for independence from Mexico. John was a member of the Texas Congress and Secretary of War for the Republic. William was a member of the Texas Senate and the first Texas Minister to the United States.

The earliest settlers here were mostly planters. Many of them brought slaves with them, and the population of the county in the 1850s was about 500 whites and more than 1,200 slaves.

1) Wharton County began and largely remains an agricultural county. It has, however, been rendered more prosperous by the finding of oil reserves as well as sulphur. So it is that oil derricks are as familiar to some pastures as 2) windmills are to others.

The present courthouse in Wharton was built in 1889. There is a Greek restaurant called Pier 59 on the bank of the Colorado — right alongside the bridge on old U. S. 59 in Wharton, with a nice view of the river.

El Campo is the largest city in Wharton County. It is also on U. S. Highway 59. There was no El Campo until 1881. The railroad came through then and established a siding and shipping point. It was called Prairie Switch in the beginning, but cattlemen began camping at the site, and the name El Campo evolved. It is Spanish for camp. Swedes, Germans and Czechs were among the early settlers, and many of the present residents preserve and carry on the customs of their ancestors' homelands.

3

3) Wharton's present courthouse dates back to the 19th Century and its downtown district 4) contains many store fronts typical of small city building styles of the period after World War I. One of its best-known native sons is TV Newsman Dan Rather. 5) Early mansions, in Wharton as elsewhere, sometimes draw camera crews as well as tourists. This old Wharton house, at 219 Burleson, was where the 1963 motion picture, "Baby, the rain must fall" was filmed.

4

5

1) El Campo dates back only to the 1880s, so it is not old by Wharton County standards, yet it has preserved some of its fine older homes. This one was built during the World War I period. 2) Texas Gulf Sulphur operates from the world's largest sulphur deposit at Newgulf. 3) The El Campo Chamber of Commerce operates this Big Game Museum on East Jackson Street in the downtown area.

The El Campo Chamber of Commerce operates a Big Game Museum in the old El Campo Clinic building on East Jackson Street downtown. On display are trophies collected by Dr. E. A. Weinheimer on various expeditions to Africa and Alaska. The museum is open every day except Saturday, and it is free.

The Historical Museum at 203 Monsarette in El Campo is open by appointment, and there is no charge.

Two buildings that attract the attention of travelers through Egypt, Texas, are 4) the aged post office building, which also sells gas, and 5) the restored old Heard home and museum. It is maintained by a descendant of W.J.E. Heard who founded Egypt in the 1830s.

Newgulf is the site of the biggest sulphur deposit in the world. The Texas Gulf Company is the operator here. The company ships sulphur all over the world. In earlier days, most of the company's employees lived in company houses in the company town. Some still do, but many employees now commute to work from homes they own themselves.

Egypt was not settled by Egyptians, and as far as we know there are no Egyptians here yet. Egypt supposedly got its name as a result of making a good grain crop and supplying food to surrounding areas during an early drought. The town was founded in the 1830s by W.J.E. Heard. He later served as a captain at San Jacinto, and one of his descendants maintains a museum in the Heard home at Egypt, where Farm Road 102 and Farm Road 1161 meet. George Northington III is the operator. There is no charge for admission to the museum.

1) *The Danish Hall at Danevang on State Highway 71 has a marker with the names of pioneer families who settled the area in the 19th Century. This is of much interest to those interested in genealogy. Many descendants of the pioneers still live in the area. 2) This monument to Shanghai Pierce is located in Howley Cemetery off Highway 35 outside Blessing. Pierce came to Texas as a ship stowaway from Rhode Island, developed his own herd of cattle, fought in the Civil War and resumed his cattle business here later. He never lived to see his favorite theory proven: That imported Brahman cattle from India would thrive in the Texas climate, and have a major impact on the U.S. livestock industry.*

Danevang on State Highway 71 at the southern end of the county was settled by Danes in 1904. There are Danish feasts and festivals periodically at the Danish Hall here. The name is Danish for "flat place where Danes live." The place is no flatter than the rest of the coast, and no less flat, either.

There is no museum preserving the legend of one of this area's most colorful oldtime residents. But the legend of Shanghai Pierce lives on, anyway.

3

4

3) It was Shanghai Pierce's fond hope that this building, erected as a hotel, would be the nucleus of his new Texas city, Pierce. It didn't work out that way. The old building is still here and still used by the Pierce Estate but it is not a hotel, nor is there a city at Pierce. 4) The Pierce Ranch today operates from this headquarters.

Pierce's name was Abel Head Pierce, and there are several stories about how he came to be called Shanghai. He came to Texas in 1854 as a stowaway on a ship from Rhode Island. He started working for a rancher at Lavaca and built up a herd of his own before he went away to fight with the Confederate Army in the Civil War. He started over after the war. He operated on the open range until he and his brother, Jonathon, founded their Rancho Grande in Wharton County near where the town of Pierce is today. The town was established when the railroad came through. Shanghai Pierce planned to build another railroad to intersect the one put through by the New York, Texas and Mexico line. He laid out a townsite and put up a hotel. The building is still standing, but it was never needed. Shanghai suffered some heavy business reverses. He died without ever building the intersecting railroad, and Pierce never became a city.

1) After Shanghai Pierce's death his Estate, and later other Texas ranches, imported Indian Brahman cattle to the U.S. When mated with domestic breeds, the resulting crossbred cattle display such "hybrid vigor" that this type breeding program is now standard practice at some of the country's largest cattle operations. 2) Mexican rancher Martin de Leon founded the settlement on the banks of the Guadalupe River which later became Victoria. He died before the Texas Revolution began and most of his colonists went to the Texas side in the fighting of 1835 and 1836.

In Shanghai's day, Texas cattle were plagued with a fever caused by a tick. Pierce did a lot of traveling and studying and concluded that Brahman cattle might be immune to the Texas tick. He died before he could prove his case, but his estate imported Brahmans from India. And Shanghai Pierce gets the credit for what was a major advance in the Texas livestock industry.

The Pierce Ranch is still operating, but it is off the road and not open to the public. You can see the place where Pierce planned to build his town though. His hotel stands right alongside U. S. Highway 59 between Wharton and El Campo.

VICTORIA COUNTY

The present city and county of Victoria grew out of a Mexican settlement established on the banks of the Guadalupe River in 1824 by Mexican rancher Martin de Leon.

De Leon died in 1833, but his colonists mostly sided with the Texas revolutionaries in 1835 and 1836. Mexican General Jose Urrea treated them as enemies when he came through with his army in 1836, but after San Jacinto some Texas zealots and

3

3) *Victoria County's ornate courthouse was built in 1892. It reflects the monumental use of stone that many municipalities in Texas sought to achieve in that period. 4) The McNamara-O'Connor Historical and Fine Arts Museum in Victoria preserves art and furnishings of 19th Century Texas. It is housed in one of the city's historically important homes.*

4

opportunists accused the Victorians of being Mexican sympathizers. Office holders with Spanish names were removed from office, and some were put off their property.

Victoria County was one of the original counties established by the Congress of the Republic in 1836 with the city of Victoria as the county seat. The present courthouse was built in 1892.

St. Mary's Catholic Church was established at 100 W. Church Street shortly after the first Mexican colonists arrived in 1824. The present building was built in 1903.

The McNamara-O'Connor Historical and Fine Arts Museum in the old McNamara-O'Connor Home at 502 North Liberty Street houses furnishings, photographs and documents from the early days and an art collection. It is open every day except Monday and Saturday, and there is no charge.

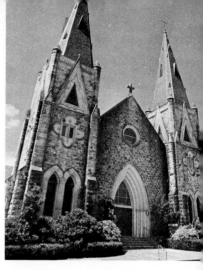

1) *The earliest church in Victoria was St. Mary's Catholic Church, established on this site when the first colonists came in 1824. This church building was built on the same site in 1903.* 2) *A number of fine old homes have been preserved in Victoria and are being maintained as private residences, including this one at 604 North Craig.*

2

An old grist mill is preserved in Town Park at 406 E. Commercial. This mill was built in 1870 at Spring Creek, using mill stones imported from Germany in 1860. The mill was moved to this site to be preserved in the 1930s. The Texas Zoo in Riverside Park specializes in animals native to Texas.

Victoria has a number of old homes still standing. Some of the addresses are 604 N. Craig, 705 N. Craig, and 307 S. Bridge, but these are private homes and not open to the public.

The French explorer LaSalle established a base in what is now

3

3) In early Texas, the wind furnished much of the energy to
grind corn and raise water, and
this restoration of an early grist
mill is reminiscent of European
windmills of the last century. It
was built in 1870 at Spring Creek
and moved to its present site, for
preservation, in the 1930s.

Victoria County back in 1685. Most of the evidence indicates it
was unintentional. The area was occupied only by Indians at the
time, but it was all claimed by Spain. LaSalle had explored the
Mississippi earlier, and he had a commission from the King of
France to establish a colony at the mouth of the Mississippi in the
territory he had named Louisiana.

LaSalle sailed for Louisiana with four ships and about 300
colonists. He lost one ship on the way over and then apparently
missed the mouth of the Mississippi and landed in Matagorda Bay.
One of his captains defected and sailed his ship back to France.
LaSalle was left with two ships. One of those was wrecked trying
to enter Matagorda Bay. The other was wrecked in the bay a few
months later, and the French colonists were left without a ship.
They used the materials from their wrecked ships to build a camp
on the banks of Garcitas Creek. LaSalle called it Fort St. Louis.
He made several trips from here with small parties trying to locate
the Mississippi. He was eventually killed by one of his own men
on one of those trips. That is believed to have happened about
where Navasota is now. A handful of his men made it back to
France by way of Canada, but most of the LaSalle colonists were
killed by disease and Indian attacks. A few survivors were rescued
by a Spanish expedition sent to find out what the Frenchmen
were up to. There is a state marker at the approximate site of
Fort St. Louis at the intersection of U. S. 59 and Farm Road 444.

The Spanish hastened to establish a mission and a presidio near
where LaSalle's fort had been, to reinforce their claim to the area.

The Mission Nuestra Senora del Espiritu Santo de Zuniga and
the Presidio Nuestra Senora de Loreto were later moved to a spot
on the Guadalupe River. This place is still called Mission Valley.
Some ruins and the remains of an irrigation dam were still visible
in the area in the 1940s. They have all disappeared now. Mission
Valley is located where Farm Road 236 meets Farm Road 237.
The mission and presidio were on what is now the Box-IN Ranch.

It is believed that the priests at this mission may have been the

1

Monuments record much of the history of South Texas. 1) This monument immortalizes a mistake. It is at Indianola and shows the French explorer LaSalle. He probably never intended to come to Texas at all and was killed following an abortive attempt to found and maintain a fort on Garcitas Creek. 2) The marker is on the site of LaSalle's short-lived Fort St. Louis. 3) Here lies William Sutton at Evergreen, last victim of the famous Sutton-Taylor feud in South Texas. There were several gun battles before the Taylors ended the feud by shooting William.

2

first to introduce livestock to Texas. Their mission and the presidio were later moved west to Goliad.

The Evergreen Cemetery at Victoria shelters the remains of many early residents originally buried somewhere else. Union troops destroyed a number of headstones and monuments in the City Cemetery and St. Mary's Churchyard during the Reconstruction Era after the Civil War, and some remains were moved from those cemeteries to Evergreen.

The last victim of a famous Texas feud is buried at Evergreen. William Sutton helped capture an alleged cattle thief named Charles Taylor in 1866. Taylor supposedly tried to escape and Sutton shot him. Taylor's relatives swore to get revenge. Buck Taylor challenged Sutton, and Sutton shot him to death, too. Other people joined in. There were several gun battles. The U. S. Military Governor of Texas finally declared open season on the Taylors. But they persisted. Sutton was boarding a ship at Indian-

4) *The grave of Victoria founder Martin de Leon, in Evergreen Cemetery, is surrounded by those of his children. Empresario de Leon saw the possibilities for stock raising on his first visit to Texas in 1805, later got a government land grant that brought his and 41 other families to the site of Guadalupe Victoria. Not all his colonists were Mexican. Some were from Ireland, Louisiana and the United States.*

ola to leave Texas for good when two Taylors stepped up and shot him to death. That ended the feud.

JACKSON COUNTY

Jackson County is another original Texas county, established by the Texas Congress in 1836. The area had previously been a Mexican municipality with the same name. It was named for U. S. President Andrew Jackson.

Members of Stephen F. Austin's colony settled here early, and they were among the early advocates of independence from Mexico. But the early settlers had less to do with the way the county developed than the railroads did.

A town named Santa Anna near the junction of the Navidad and Lavaca Rivers was the principal settlement in the area in the beginning. The settlers changed the name of the town to Texana when they changed their opinion of Santa Anna and Texana was designated the county seat after the revolution. Texana was a flourishing river port with several steamboats a week. There is nothing left now but a marker on FM Loop 1822 about ten miles south of Edna. It will be relocated when the Palmetto Bend Reservoir is completed. The first railroad to enter the county passed Texana by. The railroad took over the business the steamboats had been handling. The people moved to the railroad and built the town they eventually named Edna. It became the county seat for Jackson County in 1883.

1) *Macaroni Station, which later became Edna, got its name because an investor brought laborers from Italy to help build a railroad through this part of Jackson County. This rail line — the New York, Texas and Mexican Railroad — was never completed but its 92 miles of track did help open portions of South Texas to movement of freight and passengers. In 1885 it was incorporated into the Southern Pacific system.*

2) *A state marker in front of the Jackson County Courthouse at Edna tells how local residents voted for, then supported secession and Civil War in the 1860s. They provided crops, commodities, munitions and strategies to keep Union ships away from shore. Pioneering efforts to launch some towns in Texas met with great success. Others 3) like Francitas failed to grow.*

112

4) *General Albert Sidney Johnston, the famous Civil War general, first achieved fame as a young soldier in Texas. After the Republic was established, he fought a famous duel with Felix Huston at Camp Independence near Edna. Johnston was wounded but recovered to serve in two more wars and die while winning the Battle of Shiloh in 1862.*

The present courthouse was built in 1953.

There was not much to Edna in the beginning except a commissary catering to the men building the railroad. The railroad workers were mostly Italians. For a while the place was known as Macaroni Station.

The Texana Museum and Library at 403 North Wells in Edna is open Wednesday, Thursday and Friday afternoons and Saturday mornings. The railroad made Edna a city. Ganado is another town created by a railroad. It was a small station on the Galveston, Harrisburg and Austin line when the railroad put on an advertising campaign and ran some excursion trains for prospective land buyers. That was in 1891, and it worked. A number of Scandanavians bought land and established farms. They were hard workers and good citizens, and the railroad profited. Ganado has been profiting ever since.

Francitas is a town where the land promoters failed. It was a small town on the St. Louis, Brownsville and Mexico Railroad when some promoters decided in 1909 to turn it into a metropolis. The promoters put out ads claiming Francitas was a garden spot. They built a hotel, and they held a public sale of town lots. There were some buyers. But every town on every railroad could not be a boom town. Francitas was not.

The Palmetto Bend Reservoir in Jackson County should be completed by the fall of 1979. The reservoir will cover 11,500 acres. The Parks Department will develop a major park on the lake five miles east of Edna on State Highway 111. The park will be named Brackenridge State Park because it will be near the site of the original home of George Brackenridge. He was the same George Brackenridge who gave Brackenridge Park to the city of San Antonio. He and his sister, Mary, are buried in a secluded cemetery here near where the Brackenridge State Park will be.

The army of the Republic of Texas was largely idle after the Battle of San Jacinto. Part of the army was stationed at Camp Independence, about four miles southwest of where Edna is today. The army was briefly commanded by General Felix

1) *When early Texas communities built jails, they meant business. They intended to keep the culprits behind bars so some jails, like this early one at Port Lavaca, look a little like impregnable castles. Today, this is the Calhoun County historical museum.*

Huston. He wanted to continue the war against Mexico. President Sam Houston disagreed, and Huston was ordered to hand over command of the army to General Albert Sidney Johnston. Huston took offense at that, and he challenged Johnston to a duel. They shot it out near Camp Independence. Huston wounded Johnston and Johnston never took over the command. Both men evidently were forgiven. Both of them later led troops of the Republic in campaigns against the Indians. Johnston went on to become a general of the Confederate Army. He was killed while winning the Battle of Shiloh.

CALHOUN COUNTY

The early settlers of this state made many miscalculations and bad guesses in choosing locations for towns and ports. There were about as many mistakes in Calhoun County as anywhere. Calhoun County has bays on three sides. The county includes Matagorda Island. It has miles of low exposed coast. A lot of lives and property were lost before people learned about the damage Gulf hurricanes can do.

Calhoun County was established in 1846. It includes areas that originally were included in Victoria, Jackson and Matagorda counties.

Lavaca was originally designated the county seat. The county government was moved to Indianola in the 1850s and then moved back to Lavaca after Indianola was abandoned in 1886. Lavaca is

2

3

2) Indianola was a principal Texas port from 1844 to the 1870s and, as an early sketch suggests, it faced directly on the water. This proved its undoing as hurricanes in 1875 and 1886 crippled, then demolished it. All that remains today is the historical marker 3) which tells of Indianola's past glories and untimely end.

now known as Port Lavaca. The present courthouse was built in 1959.

The old County Jail at 301 South Ann Street houses the county's historical museum. Much of the history of Calhoun County concerns the rise and fall of Indianola.

A state marker is about all there is to show where one of the prosperous ports of the Texas coast once stood. Prince Carl of Solms-Braunfels landed here with about 100 German immigrant families in 1844. The Prince built a house, and his settlers camped here during the months it took him to negotiate the deal for the settlement that was to become New Braunfels. The Germans moved on then, but the place where they'd camped became a town and a port.

1

1) *A town named Saluria once existed here at Pass Cavallo, leading to Matagorda Bay. Confederate forces built Fort Esperanza here during the Civil War, then destroyed both fort and town when Union troops invaded in 1863. Only the foundations of the old Coast Guard station that subsequently occupied the site remain today.*

Wharves were built a half mile out into Matagorda Bay. Indianola could accommodate larger ships than Lavaca, and the location was handier. The shipping business moved to Indianola. The population did, too, and the county government followed.

When the U. S. Army conducted its great experiment in 1856 to find out whether camels would be better mounts than horses for soldiers operating in the southwestern desert, the Army's imported camels landed at Indianola.

A hurricane damaged the port in 1875. Another storm hit in 1886. That second one started a fire that destroyed much of what the storm itself did not destroy. That was the end of Indianola. What was left was abandoned. Most of the ruins have been washed away or covered up by sand.

A town called Saluria was established about 1847 at the north end of Matagorda Island at Pass Cavallo. This is the entrance to Matagorda Bay. Saluria was a resort and a port and trading center.

Confederate forces built Fort Esperanza during the Civil War to protect Saluria and the pass, but there never was a battle fought here. The Confederate troops destroyed the town of Saluria and the fort and withdrew to the mainland when a Union invasion force showed up in 1863.

The Union troops occupied Indianola and Lavaca for about six months. Neither Saluria nor Fort Esperanza was ever rebuilt. You can still make out foundations of the old Coast Guard station.

2) Port O'Connor is one city that has survived all the Gulf hurricanes up to now, although Hurricane Carla did much damage in 1961. This house 3) is widely known in Port O'Connor as the "mail order" house. It floated off its foundations during Carla but the owners found their house and put it back. It is an early pre-fab house which was ordered, disassembled, from Sears Roebuck.

Port O'Connor was established in 1910 at the southeastern tip of the mainland section of Calhoun County. It was laid out and designed to be a summer beach resort and named for the rancher the developers bought the land from. The developers put in a railroad and ran excursions and offered special deals and lots of promises.

Port O'Connor gets some protection from Matagorda Island, but not much. It has been damaged several times by storms including the vicious Carla in 1961. One house that has stood here through all the storms is the one occupied by Agnes Munsch Valigura. Her house is an early pre-fab model. Her father bought it from Sears Roebuck and assembled it himself.

1

1) *When established in 1910, Port O'Connor was billed as a coming summer beach resort, and developers did all they could to sell real estate on that basis. As it has turned out, the area is better known for fishing. It is home base for a part of the Gulf shrimp fleet and a lure to sports fishermen who come from distant points in summer and winter.*

Port O'Connor is not the resort the promoters promised it would be. But it is a base for part of the Gulf shrimp fleet and a very popular base for offshore fishing expeditions.

Calhoun County has spots to tempt fishermen of all degrees, including the Port Lavaca Park. The State Highway Department built a new bridge a few years ago to carry State Highway 35 across Lavaca Bay from Point Comfort to Port Lavaca. The State Parks and Wildlife Department took over the old bridge and turned it into a fishing pier. Children under 13 fish free here. Young people between 13 and 17 pay 50¢ and adults pay $1.00 a day for a spot on the bridge. There is a boat ramp and provision for camping nearby.

Texas resident sports fishing license fees for salt and freshwater are $4.50 per year (August 31 through August 31). Residents under 17 and over 65 are exempt, and they can fish free in Texas waters. The sports fishing license for nonresidents (salt and freshwater) is $10.50, and there are no exemptions. Nonresidents can get a temporary sports fishing license, good for five days in freshwater, for $4.50. There are no exemptions. There is also a three-day saltwater sport fishing license available to nonresidents for $1.25. Licenses may be obtained at almost any sporting goods store or bait camp in the state.

2) When the Texas State Highway Department built a new bridge to carry traffic across Lavaca Bay on State Highway 35, it turned over the old bridge to the state's Parks and Wildlife Department, and that's why Calhoun County now has perhaps the longest 'fishing pier' in Texas. It is called Port Lavaca Park.

The Air Force operated a base on Matagorda Island during World War II, and then used the place as a bombing range for several years after that. Some members of Congress claimed that the Air Force really had turned the island base into a plush hunting and fishing retreat for military officials and their guests. The base has been declared surplus by our Defense Department now. The state may get part of it for a park.

MATAGORDA COUNTY

This is another original county, established by the Texas Congress in 1836. It had been a Mexican municipality, and it was part of the original Stephen F. Austin colony. There was a cotton gin working here as early as 1825.

The town of Matagorda was the original county seat. The county government moved inland to Bay City after a storm damaged Matagorda in 1894.

Matagorda was established at the mouth of the Colorado River in 1829 as a port for the Austin colony. The Christ Episcopal Church here is said to be the oldest Episcopal church in Texas. The church was founded in 1838. (Nobody could profess to be an Episcopalian in Texas before April 21, 1836. The Spanish and

119

1) There was an Episcopal Church here as early as 1838 when the oldest of that denomination's Texas churches was founded at Matagorda. This building has been occupied by Christ Episcopal Church since 1856. 2) The salty winds that whip across Matagorda from the Gulf can quickly weather wood and timbers. This old house, after decades of exposure, is a candidate for either restoration or oblivion.

3

3) *For half a century, this building was the Matagorda Post Office, and it also served as a store. Now it has been moved to the city's park and turned into a historical museum. In the early days of the Texas Republic mail routes were sold to contractors on a bid basis. Winning bidders would then subcontract with other individuals for actual mail delivery. Those to whom the Texas Republic owed money for mail service could take it out in land — at 50 cents an acre.*

Mexican colonization laws required all settlers to be Catholics.) Christ Episcopal has been in this building since 1856.

The Matagorda Post Office operated for 50 years in an old store building owned by John Clauder. The store building has been moved to the town park, and it is now a museum.

The streets here are wide and quiet. You can tell this is a town that has been more than it is.

You can get some idea of what life was like in the old frame resort hotels that lined the Texas beaches in the 80s and 90s by visiting the Luther Hotel in Palacios. The Luther opened for business in 1903 as the Palacios Hotel. The name was changed in the Thirties. There are many fancier hotels on the coast, but the Luther has a loyal corps of winter visitors from northern states and Canada. It is open the year around and busy in the summer, too. It would be advisable to have a reservation. The Luther has no dining room.

Palacios is also the home of the Texas Baptist Encampment. Palacios is on State Highway 35. The entrance to the Baptist Encampment is on First Street. The Luther Hotel is on South Bay Boulevard.

1

1) The Texas Baptist Encampment has its home at Palacios. 2) The Luther Hotel is another Palacios landmark. Many resort hotels like this once lined the Gulf Coast beaches of Texas. The Luther opened in 1903 and many people have been coming to stay at the Luther every winter. It is on South Bay Boulevard.

2

3

3) The town of Blessing almost was named Thank God, so thankful was a prominent rancher when he learned that the railroad was coming by his ranch. He finally agreed to settle on a less exuberant name.

The town of Blessing north of Palacios supposedly got its name because an early rancher was so thankful to see the railroad reach his place. The rancher was Shanghai Pierce's brother, Jonathon. They say he wanted to name his town "Thank God" but decided on Blessing after he got over the initial excitement.

The present Matagorda County Courthouse in Bay City was built in 1965, so it is one of the newest and most modern in the state. The courthouse sits over a gas well, and most of Bay City sits on top of a gas field.

The Matagorda County Historical Museum is about a block from the courthouse at 1824 Sixth Street. It is free and open every afternoon except Monday and Saturday.

Fishermen have easy access to Matagorda County's bays and beaches. There are several boat ramps along Farm Road 2031 between Matagorda and the mouth of the Colorado.

The Intracoastal Waterway cuts along the edge of the Matagorda County coast. The waterway is a protected channel for tug and barge traffic, and it extends all the way from Brownsville to Florida. If you like to watch tugs and barges go by, you can do it at the bridge on Farm Road 2031 at Matagorda or at the bridge at the end of Farm Road 457 at Sargent's Beach.

1) Today's modern Matagorda County Courthouse, built in 1965, is in Bay City. Originally the county seat was in Matagorda, facing the Gulf. It was moved to Bay City when a storm swept across Matagorda in 1894. This is another of the original Texas counties, having been a Mexican municipality before. 2) The Matagorda County Historical Museum is a short walk from the court house. This part of the city sits atop a sizeable natural gas field, giving residents some assurance of energy supplies for the immediate future.

3

3) Traffic on the Intracoastal Waterway moves along Matagorda's coastline, adjacent to the Gulf and protected from all but the most violent weather. It can be used to go all the way from Florida to Brownsville and while used primarily by commercial traffic, many pleasure boats and fishermen find the waterway a convenient channel. Most of the commercial traffic on the 421 miles of the waterway in Texas is composed of petroleum and petroleum products. In recent years it has been also used for the movement of space vehicles to and from Texas.

The Corpus Christi Area

Nueces, Aransas, Refugio, Goliad, Bee, Live Oak,
San Patricio, Jim Wells and Kleberg counties

This part of the Texas Coast has some of the finest fishing and
some of the best recreation spots in the state. The products here
are oil and gas, cattle, cotton and grain. This part of Texas trains
more jet pilots for the Navy than any other area in the country.

NUECES COUNTY
Nueces County was created in 1846 from part of San Patricio
County. Corpus Christi has been the county seat from the begin-
ning. The present courthouses were built in 1914 and 1977.

The name Corpus Christi was originally applied to the bay at
the mouth of the Nueces River by the Spanish in 1766. They
knew about the area long before that, but they only made a
half-hearted effort to settle it. It might almost be said that the
U.S. Army started the city of Corpus Christi.

The Republic of Texas and Mexico continued to dispute over
the ownership of the land between the Nueces River and the Rio
Grande after Texas Independence was established. Texas claimed
to the Rio Grande. Mexico claimed that the boundary was the
Nueces. There was nothing where Corpus Christi is today except a
trading post operated by a freewheeling adventurer named H. L.
Kinney. He had his headquarters on a site that is now 401 North
Broadway.

Texas joined the United States in 1845, and the United States
immediately adopted the Texas claim to the territory between
the Nueces and the Rio Grande. General Zachary Taylor landed
at Corpus Christi with an Army that would a little later get
involved in skirmishes and a war with the Mexicans. Taylor's men

Nueces County was created in 1846 from part of San Patricio County. The
name was taken from the Nueces River which flows along the northern
border. Nueces is the Spanish word for nuts. Chief industries here are
petroleum, agriculture and livestock. 1) More than 470 million barrels of
oil have been pumped from the county and from offshore operations like
this one since 1930. 2) Agriculture produces an average annual income of
$22 million for Nueces County, 80% of it from this kind of grain sorghum.

3) The county's livestock industry includes beef, dairy cattle, hogs and poultry. This pasture typifies the area's coastal topography. 4) Disagreement over the Texas/Mexico border raged between the two parties long after Texas had established its independence. Texans felt their border extended to the Rio Grande River while Mexicans argued it stopped at the Nueces. The United States entered the argument when Texas was admitted to statehood in 1845 and sent General Zachary Taylor and troops into the disputed territory. Taylor established this tent city near the present site of Corpus Christi. It vanished when the troops moved on to Mexico.

initially built only a tent city here. But Corpus Christi became a shipping point for the military operation, and it soon became a town and then a city and then a major deepwater port. It has been an important military base from the very beginning.

The U. S. Navy has one half of all the air training bases it owns situated in the Corpus Christi area. The big U. S. Naval Air Station on the south side of Corpus Christi Bay is a primary training base. Advanced Navy jet training bases are operating at Kingsville and Beeville. Also, the Army has several support operations based at the Corpus Christi Naval Air Station.

1) *The Nueces County courthouse in Corpus Christi was built in 1914. The county completed a new courthouse and put this one up for sale in 1977.*
2) *The Centennial House, built by Forbes Britton an early member of Zachary Taylor's army and later a state senator, is the oldest building still standing in Corpus Christi. It has been restored and is open to the public.*

The oldest building still standing in Corpus Christi is one built by one of Zachary Taylor's men on a lot he bought from H. L. Kinney. Forbes Britton retired from the Army to settle in Texas. He may have been the first U. S. serviceman to do that. He certainly was one of the first. U. S. servicemen have been doing it ever since.

3

4

3) Corpus Christi is a major tourist and recreational center and harbors this fleet of charter fishing boats for excursions into the Gulf. 4) The Art Museum of South Texas highlights the cultural attractions of the city which also include the Corpus Christi Museum, a symphony orchestra and a little theater group. This museum is one of the city's most striking buildings.

Britton became a merchant and he served two terms in the State Senate. His big home was used as a hospital during the Civil War. It has been restored by the Corpus Christi Area Heritage Society. It is usually open on Sunday and Wednesday afternoons and by special appointment. There is a small fee. The Britton home is called Centennial House, and the address is 411 North Broadway.

The Corpus Christi Museum at 1919 North Water Street is open every afternoon except Mondays. There is no admission charge. The displays here cover history and natural history, some archeology and a big shell collection.

The Art Museum of South Texas at 1902 North Shoreline is open every day except Mondays, and there is no admission charge here.

Corpus Christi has a full range of accommodations from modest to expensive. Charter fishing boats operate from several places in the area including the public piers on Shoreline Drive within walking distance of several hotels and motels. Rates for fishing excursions in the bay run around $5.00 per person plus $2.00 for tackle and bait.

1

2

1) Accommodations for tourists at Corpus include many waterfront hotels built for easy access to the beach and the Gulf. 2) The old Tarpon Inn has hundreds of tarpon scales tacked to the interior walls. 3) The scales are from fish caught by the guests of the inn and include a personally autographed specimen from a catch President Franklin Roosevelt made in the 1930s.

4

5

4) *Nueces County Park borders* 5) *the Padre Island National Seashore on the north. Cameron County maintains a similar park on the southern end of the island. But there is some land on both sides of the island under private or corporate ownership. The Nueces County Park features shelters from the sun and the Bob Hall Fishing Pier.*

Nueces County includes most of Mustang Island but only part of the city of Port Aransas at the northern tip of the island. Part of Port Aransas is in Aransas County, and part of it is in San Patricio County. This is a major base for sport and commercial fishing.

The offshore charter fishing boats based here go out 40 to 60 miles. Such a trip will cost about $60 a person if there is a party of two, or less if there are more in the party.

You can get to Port Aransas by the causeway from Corpus Christi or by the ferry from Aransas Pass.

The old Tarpon Inn at Port Aransas is one of the landmarks on the Texas coast. It has been a hangout for tarpon fishermen since 1886. The Inn has been rebuilt a couple of times, and most of the present building dates from 1924. They have a custom of collecting and exhibiting scales from tarpon the guests have caught. One

1

1) *Mustang Island State Park was only recently acquired by the state so few improvements have been made to date but campers will find miles of uncrowded beaches where they can park for free as long as they like. 2) Nothing remains today of the original seat of government for Aransas County but Aransas City was once a thriving seaport. In 1839 it was incorporated with a customhouse for the Republic of Texas. The town of Lamar was founded in 1839 just across the channel at Lookout Point and immediately began a rivalry with Aransas City for its customhouse. Town officials of Lamar convinced Republic President Mirabeau B. Lamar to move the customhouse to their side of the channel as they had 20 houses under construction and more than double Aransas City's 500 population. Over bitter protests of officials of Aransas City, the customhouse was moved. The county seat was moved to Refugio in 1840 and Aransas City had all but disappeared by 1847.*

2

of the scales decorating the wall here came from a tarpon caught by President Franklin Roosevelt in the 1930s.

Mustang Island State Park is 14 miles south of Port Aransas. The State acquired this park only recently. There have been no improvements made yet. The park covers 2,500 acres. You can camp free on the beach.

Nueces County maintains a park on north Padre Island on the route to the Padre Island National Seashore.

The Bob Hall Fishing Pier is one of the features of the county park.

There is increasing commercial and resort development on this end of Padre Island and also at the southern end. But the Padre Island National Seashore stretches for 67½ miles. This much of the island will remain in something like its natural state forever.

3

There is no charge for admission. You can camp free on the beach. Camping in designated camping areas costs $2.00 per night.

Padre Island took its name from Father Nicolas Balli. Padre Balli got the island as a grant from the King of Spain in 1800 and it passed on to his nephew. The last Balli left in 1844, and the next resident was John Singer. He was shipwrecked here in 1847. He built a home on the ruins of the Balli place and did some ranching. He left during the Civil War because he was a Union sympathizer. One of the persistent rumors about Padre Island is that John Singer inherited part of the sewing machine fortune from his brother and buried it in the sands of Padre Island when he left. This is just a rumor, but old Spanish coins have been found on the island, and it is well established that a Spanish treasure fleet was wrecked off the lower coast of this island in the 16th Century. Some of the lost treasure was discovered by free-lance treasure hunters a few years ago. It was impounded by the state. The Texas Antiquities Committee has catalogued the artifacts and prepared a travelling exhibit. The committee is also supervising efforts to recover more artifacts from the floor of the Gulf.

ARANSAS COUNTY

Aransas County was formed in 1871 from part of Refugio County. Rockport has been the county seat since Aransas County was established. Rockport also was the county seat of Refugio County for a brief period before Aransas County was split off. The present courthouse in Rockport was built in 1957.

The original seat of government for the whole area has disappeared completely. That was Aransas City, and it was near where

1) *The Marion Packing Company Plant, shown here as it looked in 1875, was built to service the cattle industry of Aransas County. Ships loaded their cargo from long wharves. The company disappeared long ago but gave a substantial boost to the young city of Rockport while it operated. 2) The Fulton Mansion, built by cattle baron George Fulton in 1872, was far ahead of its time and was equipped with hot and cold running water, central heat and a sewage system. Plans by the current owner, the State Parks and Wildlife Dept., call for it to be restored and opened to the public.*

3

3) This Great Blue Heron is one of nearly 500 different species of birds reported to frequent the Aransas Bay area by Connie Hager, "The Texas Bird Lady." Mrs. Hagar was a nationally famous birdwatcher in the Rockport area and the waterfront area around Rockport has been designated a bird sanctuary and named in her honor.

Rockport is today. Mexico gave James Powers and James Hewetson the right to settle Irish and Mexican Catholic immigrants on Copano Bay in 1828. They established Aransas City, and it grew to a population of more than 500. It was the principal port on the western Texas coast before Corpus Christi was established. The rise of Corpus Christi and the designation of Refugio as the county seat when the area became Refugio County reduced Aransas City to a ghost town.

Rockport today is a base for part of the Gulf shrimp fleet and a major center for commercial and sport fishermen. It started as a shipping point for cattle by-products. There was a period after the Civil War when the demand for meat was less than the demand for hides and tallow and bones. Packing plants were established at several points on the Texas coast to process the cattle. The Marion Packing Company built a large plant with wharves to accommodate the ships that carried the products to market. That era did not last long. The Marion Packing Company disappeared a long time ago, but it helped give a start to the town of Rockport.

One of the big cattlemen of that period built a mansion outside Rockport that was far ahead of its time. George Fulton built this place in 1872. He put in a water system with hot and cold running water. He installed central heat and a sewage disposal system at a time when chamber pots and outdoor privies were the rule.

The Fulton Mansion at Fulton was the headquarters building for a trailer park until the State Parks and Wildlife Department bought it recently. The Department plans to restore the old mansion and open it to the public. Fulton is a couple of miles off State Highway 35, right on Aransas Bay.

1) *The Copano Bay Causeway State Park includes six acres of recreational facilities and this fishing bridge which is open to the public. Copano Bay is an extension of Aransas Bay and was originally named Santo Domingo Bay by its discoverer. After the port was established in 1785 and named for the Copane Indians, the bay's name was changed. 2) The Goose Island State Park north of Copano Bay covers 307 acres deeded to the state by private owners in 1931-35. One of the park's live oak trees shown here is the largest in Texas and national co-champion in size.*

The waterfront area along Highway 35 around Rockport has been designated a bird sanctuary. It is named for champion bird watcher Connie Hagar of Rockport.

The State Parks and Wildlife Department has another one of those fishing bridges here, like the one outside Port Lavaca. It is the old Highway 35 bridge across Copano Bay, about five miles north of Rockport. The fees are the same as at Port Lavaca, $1.00 for adults, 50¢ for young people between 13 and 17, and children under 13 fish free. The charge is only for people actually fishing. It is not covered by the annual permit.

3) The whooping crane is an object of much concern by environmentalists and ornithologists alike. The cranes have been on the endangered species list for many years. The number of birds in existence has been declining since 1870. The birds were first noticed wintering on Blackjack Peninsula between St. Charles and San Antonio Bays in the 1930s. In 1937 the peninsula was purchased by the federal government and the 4) Aransas National Wildlife Refuge was created. In October and November of each year visitors to the refuge will see the birds returning for the winter after a 2,500-mile flight from their breeding grounds in Wood Buffalo National Park, Alberta, Canada.

4

Goose Island State Park is on Highway 35 just north of the Copano Bay Fishing Pier. Fishing, swimming, picnicking and camping are permitted. The entrance fee is $1.00 per vehicle. Campsites can be reserved by writing Goose Island State Recreation Area, Route 1, Box 105, Rockport 78382 or calling 512-729-2858.

The Aransas National Wildlife Refuge has been made famous by the whooping cranes that winter here. The Refuge is on the bay south of Austwell, and it is open to visitors. There are provisions for picnicking and camping. A large excursion boat carries visitors through part of the refuge during the period between October and April when the cranes are here.

1) *Mount Calvery Catholic Cemetary in Refugio is the final resting place of Amon B. King and his men. They were sent out by James Fannin to rescue some families stranded at Refugio during the Texas Revolution.* 2) *In 1936 the state raised this marker to honor King and his men who were killed by Mexican troops after their rescue mission. Their remains were gathered from the prairie where they were left and buried by a group of Refugio citizens. The grave was accidentally discovered many years later in what was then Mount Calvery Cemetery. They were reinterred by the state with full religious and military ceremonies in 1934.*

REFUGIO COUNTY

Refugio has a "g" in it only in the written version. The name is pronounced as though it were spelled with a "w" where the "g" is. Re-*few*-rio. Not all the Spanish names in this part of the world take Spanish pronunciations. This one does.

Refugio County grew out of the James Powers and James Hewetson colony. It was much larger before sections were taken away to form other counties. Refugio was one of the original colonies. The city of Refugio has been the county seat during most of the county's history. The present courthouse was built in 1919.

The city of Refugio was established on the site where the Spanish had earlier established the Mission Nuestra Senora del Refugio. Refugio and the old mission were the scene of one of the defeats Texans suffered in their War for Independence in the spring of 1836.

Santa Anna had overwhelmed William B. Travis' small force at the Alamo on March 6th. General Jose Urrea was marching toward Goliad to mop up the resistance there. Panic was spreading among the Anglo settlers.

140

3) *This tree on the courthouse grounds at Goliad is known as "The Hanging Tree." Legend has it that before the courthouse was built in 1894, criminals were tried under this tree before being hanged from its branches. This tree might have provided shade for James Fannin's weary men and many others during the tragic Goliad campaign.*

James Fannin was in command at Goliad. On March 10th, he sent a small force under Amon B. King to Refugio to escort several families to Goliad. King and the refugees were ambushed by Mexican irregulars. They ducked into the old Refugio mission and sent word to Fannin that they needed help. Fannin sent a party commanded by William Ward to help the King party. Ward raised the seige, but his men and King's, too, then got into a skirmish with elements of Urrea's army. King and his men were captured and executed on March 16th. Ward and his party escaped toward Victoria, but the Mexicans caught them later and marched them to Goliad and shot them along with Fannin and his men.

The Mexican Army was following the orders of the Mexican Congress in executing captured rebels instead of treating them as prisoners of war. King and his men were shot at a spot north of the old Refugio Mission, and their bodies were left there on the ground. Citizens of Refugio gathered up the bones and remains after the war was over and buried them. No record was made of where the remains were buried, but a grave containing the skeletons of 16 men was accidentally discovered in 1934 in the Mount Calvary Catholic Cemetery. The remains were identified as those of King and his men. The state put up memorial markers in 1936 in the cemetery and in a park named for King.

Refugio's problems did not end when Sam Houston defeated the Mexicans at San Jacinto. There were several Indian raids after that. The last one was a Commanche raid in 1852.

GOLIAD COUNTY

Goliad was one of the original counties established by the first Texas Congress in 1836. It is one of the most historic areas in the state. The city of Goliad has been the county seat since the county was established. The present courthouse dates from 1894. They say that before that they tried some culprits under the old tree on the courthouse grounds and hanged them from the tree.

141

1

1) The courthouse at Goliad was built in 1894 and was enlarged and modernized in 1964. Goliad County was created in 1836, organized in 1837 and named for the municipality of Goliad. It is one of the original counties of Texas. 2) The American Revolution Bicentennial Commission of Texas gave full approval to Goliad's plans for restoration and beautification of the courthouse square including this Old City Market which now houses a museum. The square has also been declared a National Preservation District and qualifies for help from the National Park Service.

2

The people of Goliad take considerable pride in their trees. They have left several of them standing in the middle of their streets, and the traffic just has to go around them.

The courthouse square has been declared a National Preserva-

3

4

3) Nuestra Senora del Espiritu Santo de Zuniga Mission, commonly called La Bahia Mission, now located just outside Goliad, was founded in 1722 near Matagorda Bay among the Coco, Cujane and Karankawa Indians. It was protected by the presidio of Nuestra Senoro de Loreto 4) which was also established to prevent any future French landings in the area. In 1727 the mission and presidio were moved to a spot on the Guadalupe River and moved again in 1749 at the request of the missionaries to this final site on the San Antonio River. The restoration of the old fort and chapel was supervised and paid for by Kathryn Stoner O'Connor in the 1960s. She was honored by King Juan Carlos I of Spain for this contribution toward preserving the Spanish heritage of Texas.

tion District so restoration work on the buildings here qualifies for help from the National Park Service.

There is an old blacksmith shop still operating at 301 East Fannin Street. There is a museum in the old City Market building at Franklin and Market, open every day except Mondays. No fee for admission, but donations are welcome.

The Spanish began settling this area in 1749 when they moved

1) *James Walker Fannin Jr. first became involved in the Texas Revolution in 1835 as captain of the Brazos Guards. He was present at the first battle of the Revolution at Gonzales and at the battle of Concepcion with James Bowie. While colonel of the Provisional Regiment of Volunteers at Goliad, Fannin was ordered by Sam Houston to retreat to Victoria but hesitated to await the return of some of his men from Refugio. When he learned those men had been captured he began his delayed retreat but he was surrounded by Jose Urrea and forced to surrender at the battle of Coleto.*

to this location the mission and presidio that had been established originally near Matagorda Bay and later moved to the Guadalupe River. The mission was Nuestra Senora del Espiritu Santo de Zuniga, and the presidio was Nuestra Senora de Loreto. They are often referred to as La Bahia mission and presidio because of their original location on the bay.

The mission is now part of Goliad State Park, on Highway 183 and 77A, about half a mile south of Goliad. The mission is open every day. The admission fee is included in the fee for admission to the park. That fee is $1.00 per vehicle. There are provisions for camping and shelters for rent. For reservations, write Goliad State Historical Park, Box 727, Goliad 77963 or phone 512-645-3405.

The Presidio is on the opposite bank of the San Antonio River, and it is now a museum. There is a small admission fee. The Presidio is one mile south of Goliad on Highway 183-77A. The Presidio is open every day except Christmas and Good Friday. It has been restored, and the museum features artifacts from the Indian and Colonial and Revolutionary Days. The Spanish

2) Fannin was honored by his fellow Texans with this monument in downtown Goliad. 3) Fannin and his men are buried near the presidio outside Goliad. When Fannin surrendered at Coleto, he thought he had struck a bargain with Urrea to take him and his men as prisoners of war and parole them to the United States as soon as possible. Urrea let Fannin believe his terms were accepted to avoid a fight to the death with Fannin's heavily armed men. In truth, Urrea knew Santa Anna had ordered all prisoners shot and while he sent token letters to Santa Anna requesting clemency he knew Fannin was doomed.

mission era was well past its peak by 1836. Many missions were already in ruins, then.

The Mission Nuestra Senora del Rosario was built in the Goliad area in 1754 to minister to the Karankawa Indians. There is nothing left of Rosario except a marker, but the state has acquired the property. It is on U. S. 59, about four miles west of Goliad. The importance of the missions had declined by 1829 to the point that the Mexican government decided to turn the

1) This cannon, now part of Fannin's memorial in downtown Goliad, helped inflict heavy damage during Fannin's last stand at Coleto. A similar cannon in nearby Gonzales was the star of an earlier drama. Colonists in Gonzales dug up that cannon from a peach orchard where they had hidden it when Mexican troops were determined to retrieve it. They loaded it with chains and scrap iron and went looking for a fight. They soon met the approaching Mexicans and used the cannon to fire the first shot of the Revolution. The battle is celebrated each October in Gonzales as "Come and Take It Days," from the motto on the Gonzales battle flag.

presidio here into a town and the town was named Goliad. It was a purely Mexican town then, but by 1835 it was swarming with Anglos bent on revolution.

The importance of Goliad and Refugio in the events leading up to the revolution resulted from their location on the most direct supply route between the coast and San Antonio. There was a port called Copano on Copano Bay just a dozen miles south of Refugio at the time.

The agitation for independence among the Texas colonists caused the Mexican military commander at Matamoros to bring a force to Copano in the winter of 1835 to find out what was going on. He was Martin Perfecto de Cos. He came to Goliad and left some supplies and a small garrison at the presidio here and went on to San Antonio. At the same time, another Mexican official was trying to compel the settlers at Gonzales to give back a cannon they had been given to use on the Indians. The settlers defied the Mexicans and fired the cannon at them, and the die was cast. There would be war. Rebels attacked the garrison at Goliad and took control of this town and then moved on to San Antonio. They forced Cos to surrender after a short siege and battle. They had his supplies cut off. He gave up on December 9th.

The rebels remained in control of Goliad and San Antonio until the following March. The Mexican armies that came north to restore order then brought their supplies with them in caravans of wagons and carts and on the backs of pack animals. The Texans were having great difficulties with their supplies and communications. General Sam Houston did not learn until March 11th that the Alamo had fallen March 6th. Houston sent word to Fannin that he'd better begin moving his force from Goliad eastward toward Victoria, forthwith. But Fannin did not get moving

2) The present courthouse for Bee County was built in 1912 at Beeville. The county was created in 1857 from parts of Karnes, Live Oak, Goliad, Refugio and San Patricio counties. The first permanent settlers were Irish. They settled here in 1826.

until March 19th. He made a rest stop about 12 miles west of Victoria on an open prairie near Coleto Creek. Jose Urrea's Mexican Army caught up with him here. Fannin's men put up a good fight, but they were badly outnumbered and surrounded. Fannin surrendered on March 20th. Urrea went through the motions of recommending to Santa Anna that the prisoners be spared. Then he dumped the responsibility on a subordinate and headed on east looking for more rebels. The subordinate had his firing squads execute Fannin and 342 other prisoners at Goliad on March 27th. The executions gave Texans their second rallying cry for the Battle of San Jacinto, three weeks later.

The Fannin Battleground is now a state park. It is one mile off U. S. 59 nine miles east of Goliad. There is a picnic pavillion but no camping.

Colonel Fannin and his troops were left where they were shot, but other Texans later gathered up the remains and buried them just southeast of the presidio grounds at Goliad. A monument marks the spot today.

People in Goliad don't spend all their time studying history and contemplating the past. They have horse racing in the spring, summer and fall at La Bahia Downs.

BEE COUNTY

Bee County was created in 1857 from parts of Karnes, Live Oak, Goliad, Refugio and San Patricio counties.

Beeville has been the county seat since the county was established, but Beeville was moved from its original location on Medio Creek to the present location in 1860. The present county courthouse was built in 1912.

1) *The McClanahan House in Beeville was the first business building in the city. The town had become a shipping center for the surrounding cattle country with the construction of the San Antonio and Aransas Pass Railway in 1886 and the Gulf, Western Texas and Pacific Railway in 1888. 2) The county seat of Live Oak County was moved to George West from Oakville in 1919. The courthouse here was built in 1918. Live Oak County was named for the groves of live oaks in the region. John McMullen and James McGloin got a Mexican grant and brought settlers here from Ireland.*

2

The county and the city were named for Barnard Bee. He played a prominent part in Texas politics during the days of the Republic. Bee was Secretary of War in Sam Houston's cabinet and Secretary of State in Lamar's cabinet. He also served for a time as Texas Minister to the United States. He was opposed to having Texas annexed to the United States, and he returned to his original home in South Carolina after the annexation was completed. Bee never knew there was a county named for him. He died in South Carolina before Bee County was formed.

This is cattle and oil country. The cattle business here was well started before the Civil War. Cattle from here walked the Chisolm trail to the markets in Kansas in the late 1860s and early 1870s. The oil was discovered first in 1929 at Pettus.

The first permanent settlers here were Irish. A family named

3) *Grace Armentrout, of George West in Live Oak County, is preserving an old caboose in the park she has given to the city. The park includes a swimming pool and an elaborate cactus garden. Mrs. Armentrout still lives here, but she has opened the park to the public.*

O'Toole came in 1826, and others followed. The Mexican government by that time was already getting leery of immigrants from the United States and considered Irish Catholics a better bet.

Jet airplanes are conspicuous in the skies around Beeville. Chase Field trains about one third of the Navy's jet pilots. The student pilots practice bombing and strafing runs on a target area west of the field.

Some other interesting buildings in Beeville are: Camp Ezell House, 1313 N. Flournoy; Cooke Home, 1001 S. Fowler; George House, 801 N. Adams; McClanahan House, 206 E. Corpus Christi (the first business building).

LIVE OAK COUNTY

Live Oak County was created in 1856 out of parts of Nueces and San Patricio counties. A community called Oakville was designated as the county seat. But the county government moved to George West in 1919 for the usual reason. George West was on the railroad and Oakville was not. The present courthouse in George West was built in 1918.

The early permanent settlers here, too, were Irish. The county was part of the colony founded by the Irish empresarios John McMullen and James McGloin. The old Mexican oxcart road to San Antonio passed through here. It was the road Santa Anna used on his way to the Alamo.

One of the citizens of George West has turned her home into a park and donated it to the city. Grace Armontrout still lives in the place, and she has reserved the right to live here as long as she likes. Her park includes a swimming pool and an elaborate cactus garden. It is open all the time and it is free.

The late writer J. Frank Dobie was born in Live Oak County, on his father's ranch, on FM 3261 southeast of George West.

The Tips State Park one mile west of Three Rivers is a pleasant

1) Tips State Park has 31 acres on the Frio River in Live Oak County. The park is a mile west of Three Rivers. It was deeded by private owners in 1925 and then leased for 99 years to Three Rivers. 2) Lake Corpus Christi, also known as Lake Lovenskiold, is an artificial lake on the Nueces River where Live Oak, San Patricio and Jim Wells counties meet. It covers 14,188 acres and supplies water to Corpus Christi.

place for a picnic. The park is a small one on the Frio River. Fishing is permitted. There are no provisions for camping.

Lake Corpus Christi is in the southeast corner of Live Oak County. There is a state park on the lower end of the lake. The park is in San Patricio County.

3

4

3) Sinton replaced San Patricio as the county seat of San Patricio County in 1893. The courthouse here was built in 1928. The county was settled by Irish families brought in by James McGloin and John McMullen. 4) The Rob and Bessie Welder Wildlife Refuge, eight miles northeast of Sinton, was created from the Welder Ranch by a provision in Rob Welder's will. It has been owned continuously by the Welder family and none of the rich soil has ever been cultivated. More than 400 subspecies of birds have been recorded in the refuge and in the immediate vicinity.

SAN PATRICIO COUNTY

San Patricio is an original county established by the first Congress of the Republic of Texas in 1836. The area had been organized as a Mexican municipality before that. The first permanent settlers were the Irish and Mexican colonists brought in by

151

1) The home of James McGloin still stands outside San Patricio, the city he founded in 1830. McGloin was a native of Ireland. It is said he missed a boat he was to take to Australia and wound up meeting John McMullen at an English port. McMullen convinced McGloin to join him in an empresario enterprise to introduce Irish colonists to Texas. They were given a grant of land along the left bank of the Nueces River and brought hundreds of families to the area. Citizens of San Patricio have begun preserving many of their old buildings including 2) St. Paul's Academy for Boys built in 1876 and 3) the McKeown home built in 1868 and now a museum.

2

3

4) Old Texas homes and business buildings are often torn down for their materials or to make way for newer buildings. The old barns and outbuildings often stand until they fall down. A surprising number of them have stood for a very long time. They have a kind of homely beauty as evidenced by this one outside San Patricio.

John McMullen and James McGloin. They named their settlement for the Irish saint, and St. Patrick's Day is always a big event in San Patricio. They have a celebration on whatever weekend is closest to March 17th.

The town of San Patricio was the original county seat. The government moved to Sinton in 1893 to get on the railroad. The present courthouse at Sinton was built in 1928.

The Welder Wildlife Refuge outside of Sinton was founded by the late San Patricio County rancher Rob Welder. When he died in 1953, he left 7,800 acres to be used for wildlife research. The Welder Foundation offers scholarships to graduate students interested in studying specific wildlife problems. There are conducted tours of the refuge every Thursday afternoon.

One of the early skirmishes of the revolution was fought around San Patricio in February of 1836. A party of revolutionaries preparing to launch a raid on Matamoros was surprised and largely wiped out by Mexican soldiers under the command of General Jose Urrea. There is a memorial marker on the grounds of the old cemetery.

153

1) *The people of Taft on U.S. 181 decorated their old railroad depot with a mural depicting some of the area's history as Taft's project for the Bicentennial Year. Taft was named for President William Howard Taft's brother, Charles. He was one of the partners in the ranch this station was built to serve.*

The only woman ever hanged in Texas was an innkeeper at San Patricio. Chipita Rodriguez was convicted of robbing and murdering a lodger at her inn. She was hanged from a tree on the bank of the Nueces River. There is a story that the tree was later destroyed by lightning. It may be only a story.

Another story that may not be anything more than a story concerns this house on Farm Road 666 outside of San Patricio. Colonizer James McGloin built this house after his partner, John McMullen, had sold out his interest in the colony and moved to San Antonio. The story is that during a party at the house one night, McGloin thought he saw the ghost of his former partner standing in a doorway, covered with blood. McGloin supposedly got on his horse and rode straight to San Antonio to check on his friend and found that he had been murdered.

The people of San Patricio have started preserving old buildings. The building that housed the St. Paul's Academy For Boys has been restored and it is now a private home. It dates from 1876. The McKeown house that was built in 1868 has been restored as a museum. It is open on Sundays.

The people of Taft on U. S. 181 decorated their old railroad depot with a mural depicting some of their area's history. This was Taft's project for the Bicentennial Year. Taft was named for

2

2) The county courthouse for Jim Wells County was built in Alice in 1949. The county was created in 1911 from Nueces County and named for James B. Wells Jr., a man famed for his skill in reducing the friction between the original Texas-Mexican settlers and the Anglo Americans who came into the area with the development of railroads and irrigation.

President William Howard Taft's brother, Charles, because he was one of the partners in the ranch this station was originally built to serve.

Lake Corpus Christi State Recreation Area is outside of Mathis at the northwestern end of San Patricio County. This is one of the Class I parks. There are provisions for camping, and there are shelters for rent. The entrance fee is $1.00 per vehicle if you do not have an annual permit. The shelters are extra. You can make reservations by writing Lake Corpus Christi State Recreation Area, P. O. Box 1167, Mathis, Texas 78368 or calling 512-547-2635.

1) *The county seat and principal city of Kleberg County is Kingsville. The courthouse here was built in 1913. Before 1890 the county was almost treeless, but since that time the portions not in cultivation have been covered with mesquite, huisache and oak. Four-fifths of the county is included in the King Ranch.*

JIM WELLS COUNTY

Jim Wells County was organized in 1911. The area previously had been part of Nueces County. This is mesquite country. Oil is the biggest business. Ranching is next, and the political wars here have often attracted statewide attention.

The county was named for J. B. Wells Jr. He was a prominent valley lawyer and developer and the son of one of the soldiers of the revolution.

Alice has been the county seat since the county was created. The present courthouse was built in 1949. Alice was named for Alice King Kleberg, daughter of rancher Richard King and the wife of rancher Robert Kleberg.

There was a fort at Sandia on State Highway 359 during the Civil War. It was a base for blockade runners bringing in supplies and hauling out cotton. The marker in Sandia says Fort Casa Blanca had walls three feet thick, but nothing is left of it today.

There is a small state park on Farm Road 70 about nine miles south of Sandia where there was a Mexican fort in colonial days. The fort was called Lipantitlan because it was in the area inhabited by the Lipan Indians. Texans won here in 1835 one of the skirmishes that preceded the revolution. Picnicking is permitted. Camping is not.

2

2) *Texas A & I University located in Kingsville was founded in 1925. The original name, South Texas Teachers College, was changed to Texas College of Arts and Industries in 1929 and to the present name in 1967. The university opened a branch in Laredo in 1970 and a branch in Corpus Christi in 1972.*

KLEBERG COUNTY

Kleberg County was organized in 1913. The area had previously been part of Nueces County. The county was named for Robert Justus Kleberg. He was a German immigrant and San Jacinto veteran and the father of the Robert Kleberg who married into the King Ranch family.

The county seat and principal city in Kleberg County is Kingsville. The present courthouse was built in 1913.

This is the home of the Texas Arts and Industries University. One of the Navy's jet training bases is located here, and there is some industry now. But Kingsville originally was just the railroad station for the King Ranch. Ranch headquarters are on State Highway 141 west of town. The ranch is not open to visitors.

The Santa Gertrudis breed of cattle was developed at the King Ranch, and Kingsville is headquarters for the Santa Gertrudis Breeders' Association. The breed was named for the original King Ranch property. Richard King bought a Spanish land grant known as Santa Gertrudis Ranch in 1852 with money he and his

157

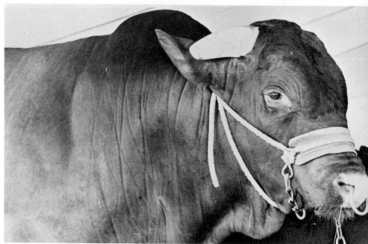

1) The King Ranch may be the most famous ranch in the world. It encompasses over a million acres of land in Nueces, Kenedy, Kleberg and Willacy counties. The running W brand became the official King Ranch symbol of ownership in the 1860s. Buying into the 2) Santa Gertrudis breeding business, originated at the King Ranch, is one way Texans with money can advance their social standing.

partner, Mifflin Kenedy, had made hauling supplies for Zachary Taylor on their steamboats. The ranch now sprawls over one million acres in Kleberg, Kenedy, Nueces and Willacy counties. The ranch raises Quarter Horses and race horses in addition to cattle and also has a large oil income.

The John E. Conner Museum on the campus of Texas A & I University has a collection of 900 cattle brands and exhibits covering natural and local history. The museum is open every day. There is no charge for admission.

There is in this county another one of those beach resorts that didn't make it. Riviera Beach on Baffin Bay was established in 1908. The town got a railroad in 1913 and a hurricane in 1916. There is not much left of the resort town today.

3

3) *Riviera Beach on Baffin Bay in Kleberg County is another beach resort that didn't make it. It was established in 1908, got a railroad in 1913 and was destroyed by a hurricane in 1916. This is all that remains today.*

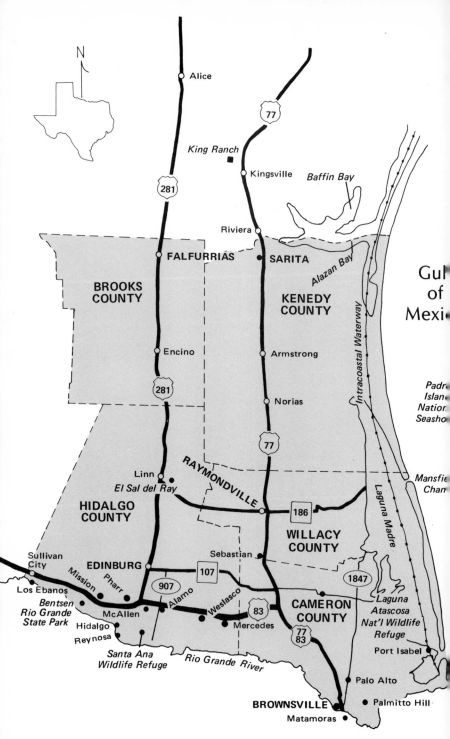

The Lower Coast
Brooks, Kenedy, Willacy, Cameron
and Hidalgo counties

BROOKS COUNTY

Brooks County was established in 1911, taking in areas that had previously been in Hidalgo, Starr and Zapata counties. The present courthouse at Falfurrias was built in 1911.

Falfurrias has been the county seat since the county was established. The town is much older. It was established in 1883 by rancher Edward C. Lasater. Falfurrias is an Indian word meaning "Heart's Delight."

Brooks County was named for James A. Brooks. He was a captain of the Texas Rangers. He served in the Legislature and was the first county judge of Brooks County.

The Heritage Museum at Falfurrias has a special collection of materials and documents and photographs relating to the history of the Texas Rangers in addition to displays on the history of the county and the livestock industry. It is located at 24 St. Mary's Street and is open weekdays and Saturday mornings. It is free.

Ranching, oil and gas are the big industries here, but there is some irrigation and farming.

Falfurrias butter comes from the creamery Edward Lasater established here in 1909.

KENEDY COUNTY

Kenedy was one of the last counties to be established. It was created in 1925 from parts of Cameron, Hidalgo and Willacy counties and named for Richard King's ranching partner, Mifflin Kenedy.

1) The town of Falfurrias dates back to 1883. Rancher Edward C. Lasater founded it. The Brooks County courthouse was built here in 1911. This is mostly an agricultural economy with ranching and irrigated farming the most visible industries. 2) Roadside fruit and vegetable stands are evidence of the county's agricultural heritage although oil and gas make a contribution to the area's income, too.

3) The Kenedy County courthouse at Sarita is surrounded by a fence and not just for decoration. It is designed to keep the cows out. Cattle are most important to this county. Most of the land in the county is taken up by private ranches. Service stations are scarce.

The county seat is Sarita. The present courthouse was built in 1921. Sarita is the only town in the county. It was named for Mifflin Kenedy's granddaughter. The highway map shows a town named Norias on U. S. 77 south of Sarita, but Norias is the headquarters of the Norias section of the vast King Ranch and nothing more.

The main thing to know about Kenedy County is that you'd better enter it with enough fuel in your tank to get out again. The road maps the oil companies used to give away always warned that there were no service stations between Riviera, in Kleberg County, and Raymondville, in Willacy County. Kenedy County is almost entirely private ranches. Several of them have oil and gas wells, but service stations are scarce.

The maps also show a place named Armstrong. It is just the headquarters of the Armstrong Ranch. This is the home of Tobin and Anne Armstrong. She was the U. S. Ambassador to Britain during the Ford Administration.

1 1) Don Pedro Jaramillo, a famous Mexican-American faith healer, settled at Los Olmos near Falfurrias in 1882. People came from great distances to see him and sometimes he saw several hundred people a day. When he died in 1907 one of his followers built a small shrine over his grave. Some people come here seeking relief for their problems.

WILLACY COUNTY

Willacy County was organized in 1911 from parts of Cameron and Hidalgo counties. Raymondville has been the county seat since the beginning. The present courthouse was built in 1922. Oil and farming are the big businesses here. Tourism and fishing are big, too.

Willacy County was named for John G. Willacy. He did not live here. Willacy was representing Corpus Christi in the Legislature and he introduced the bill that created this new county. So they named it for him.

Raymondville is another one of those towns created by land and railroad promoters. It was named for E. B. Raymond. He founded the Raymond Town and Improvement Company, and the company launched the town.

The Raymondville Historical and Community Center at Harris and 7th has displays covering the history of the area and featuring some of the artifacts recovered from the water off Port Mansfield. A channel dredged through Padre Island gives Willacy County a port that is also served by the Intracoastal Waterway.

There is a salt lake near Raymondville that once supplied the Spanish colonies in Mexico with table salt. The lake is called El Sal Viejo. Some of the history is recited on the state marker on State Highway 186, about 8½ miles west of Raymondville.

2) The salt lake called *El Sal Viejo* near Raymondville, as this marker explains, has existed since the earliest Spanish explorers came through the region. It once supplied the Spanish colonies with table salt. 3) The Willacy County Courthouse at Raymondville was built in 1922. As the palm tree suggests, this is a semi-tropical climate. Many people are attracted here by the mild winters and good fishing.

4) The Raymondville Historical and Community Center preserves artifacts of the city's past and includes some items recovered from the Gulf of Mexico off Port Mansfield.

1) The Cameron County courthouse at Brownsville was built in 1914. The county itself dates back to 1848. It was named for Ewen Cameron, executed by the Mexican forces after he took part in a raid against territory claimed by Mexico.

Part of the Laguna Atascosa National Wildlife Refuge for migratory birds is on the Laguna Madre in Willacy County. It extends southward into Cameron County, too.

The town of Sebastian on U. S. 77 south of Raymondville was a stop on the stage coach line to the Rio Grande Valley in the 1860s.

CAMERON COUNTY

Cameron County was created in 1848 out of part of Nueces County. The county was named for a man the Mexicans executed in Mexico after the Revolution had ended. Santa Anna had returned to Mexico and regained the Presidency. Irregular Texas forces were still skirmishing with Mexican forces in the disputed territory between the Nueces and the Rio Grande. They sometimes also staged raids across the border into territory Texas had never claimed. Ewen Cameron went on one of those raids, and he was captured. He was executed for leading an escape attempt. Cameron was a native of Scotland.

The county seat of Cameron County is Brownsville. The present courthouse was built in 1914.

Brownsville was a fort before it was a town. General Zachary Taylor established a fort here as soon as he reached the Rio Grande in 1846 on his mission to make it plain to Mexico that the United States considered the territory it acquired with the annexation of Texas extended to the Rio Grande. One of the first men killed in fighting with the Mexicans was Major Jacob Brown, and the fort was named for him. The city was named for the fort when it was founded two years later.

2) Fort Brown at Brownsville was here before the city was established. It was named for a soldier who was killed when General Zachary Taylor's forces moved into the area in 1846 to enforce the U.S. claim that American territory extended to the Rio Grande River, not just to the Nueces. Fort Brown had a long history as a military base in 19th and 20th Century wars. The fort was taken out of service in 1945 and a part of the fort now 3) is the Texas Southmost College campus.

3

Fort Brown served as a base for Indian fighters, for guardsmen hunting bandits, for Confederate troops and Union troops, and for the 12th U. S. Cavalry in World War I and the 124th Cavalry in World War II. The fort was taken out of service in 1945 and part of it is now the campus of the Texas Southmost College.

The first two engagements of the war between the United States and Mexico and the last land battle of the Civil War were fought near Brownsville.

Mexican attacks on Zachary Taylor's troops at Palo Alto, 5½

1

1) This marker commemorates one of the first skirmishes in the Brownsville area in the war between the U.S. and Mexico. It recalls the clash at Resaca de la Palma on what is now the Pardes Leni Road. The war led finally to moving the borders of Texas to the Rio Grande and to U.S. acquisition of New Mexico and California. 2) This marker is on the site of the Battle of Palmito Hill, last battle of the Civil War, actually fought weeks after the war had ended. Confederate cavalry, not knowing the war was over, engaged Union forces who were on the way to take over Brownsville. The fight lasted several days until the Union soldiers withdrew to the protective artillery of nearby Brazos Island.

2

miles north of Brownsville on what is now Farm Road 1847, and at Resaca de la Palma on what is now Pardes Leni Road, probably were the intended result of the Taylor expedition. They brought on the U. S. declaration of war against Mexico. Taylor won both of the skirmishes and the United States won the war. In the final treaty, the U. S. got the Rio Grande established as the border and for an extra $15 million got California and New Mexico, too. There are state markers at the sites of the battles of Palo Alto and Resaca de la Palma. One of the officers serving with Zachary

3

3) *This feathered beauty is a resident of the Gladys Porter Zoo in Brownsville, where birds and animals live in natural surroundings without fences or cages. It is considered one of the outstanding zoos in Texas.*

Taylor in the Brownsville area was Jefferson Davis, later to be President of the Confederate States of America.

Union troops set out from their base on Brazos Island in May of 1865 to take over the city of Brownsville. The Federals were surprised by Confederate cavalry. There was a skirmish. It lasted a couple of days. The Union troops finally retreated back to Brazos Island. The Confederate troops didn't learn until the fight was over that the war was over before this fight began. Lee had surrendered at Appomattox a month earlier. The Union men knew it, but they didn't get a chance to explain. That Battle of Palmito Hill was fought about 12 miles east of Brownsville.

The city of Brownsville was founded by a trader named Charles Stillman. He built the first house in the new city. His house still stands at 1305 East Washington Street. It is now a museum with period furnishings and some historical displays. The Stillman House Museum is open weekdays and Sunday afternoons. There is a small fee.

The Brownsville Art League maintains a fine arts museum in a home that was built in 1836. The Art League Museum is at 230 Fort Brown.

The Gladys Porter Zoo in Brownsville is one of the outstanding zoos in Texas. It is at Ringgold and 6th Street. There is an admission fee.

This is the Magic Valley where irrigation has made rich farms

1) *The Stillman House is the restored residence of the man who founded Brownsville. Charles Stillman's house was the first house in the city. It has been turned into a museum, furnished in keeping with the period when he lived there. 2) This international toll bridge connects Brownsville with the Mexican city of Matamoros on the other side of the Rio Grande River.*

and farmers rich. The climate attracts many winter visitors and increasing numbers of retired people.

Industrial development along the channel to the port of Brownsville is increasing. And Brownsville has an international toll bridge connecting it with the Mexican city of Matamoros on the other side of the Rio Grande.

The second city in Cameron County is Harlingen. This city was founded by Lon C. Hill. He was one of the first people to see the potential in irrigating the Valley. The home Hill built as head-quarters for his plantation is now a park. It is the oldest house in

3

4

3) Tall palm trees line the wide streets of Harlingen, second largest city in Cameron County. The city's founder, Lon C. Hill, was among those who early saw the potential of irrigating the "Valley" of Texas. 4) Harlingen's Rio Grande Valley Museum is a replica of the Paso Real Stagecoach Inn on the Brownsville-San Antonio stage line.

Harlingen. It is open Tuesday afternoons and at other times by appointment. There is no charge for admission.

The Rio Grande Valley Museum in Harlingen Industrial Air Park is open every day except Mondays and Saturdays. It features displays and photographs of earlier times. There is no charge for admission, but donations are welcome. The building is a replica of the Paso Real Stagecoach Inn on the stage line between Brownsville and San Antonio. The last remaining ruins of the original inn were washed into the Arroyo Colorado by Hurricane Beulah in 1967.

The most popular museum in Cameron County is a collection of old airplanes. The Confederate Air Force is an organization of pilots and airplane buffs. The CAF has a fleet of World War II planes at Rebel Field in Harlingen. Many of them are in flying

1

1) *Examples of most of the familiar airplanes of World War II can be seen on the Confederate Air Force's Rebel Field at Harlingen. The CAF grew out of pilots and old airplane buffs' efforts to gather and restore old planes to flying condition. The CAF now does air shows all over the nation, and the Rebel Field is open to visitors. 2) Right now, Brazos Island is more island than park with little more than a few small boat wrecks to break the beach landscape. However the state has acquired some of the island and it will be developed in the future as a state park. 3) The new causeway from Port Isabel to South Padre Island provides concrete slopes for sidewalk surfers. Steady development of the area also is proving a lure for growing numbers of people who want to settle in a warmer climate.*

condition and the Confederate Air Force stages air shows all over the country. The museum at Rebel Field is open Sunday afternoon and all day every other day of the week. They ask for donations of $2.00 each for adult visitors and $1.00 each for children.

The state has acquired some beach property on Brazos Island on the south side of the entrance to the Brownsville ship channel. It is going to be developed. Right now it is undeveloped open beach, but camping is permitted.

The most popular beaches in the area are on the opposite side of the Brownsville Channel entrance, on the southern end of Padre Island. A new causeway simplifies the trip from Port Isabel. South Padre is no longer just a resort. More and more permanent residents are settling here in the sun.

2

3

1

1) *The long, flat sands of Padre Island are increasingly punctuated these days by development of residential buildings. This condominium is characteristic of modern designs that attract permanent residents and seekers of second homes. 2) Ila Loetscher is a Padre Island institution now. She came to Padre from Iowa years ago and became interested in the island's sea turtles. She has encouraged the Ridley turtles to resume laying eggs in Padre Island sands. She also has trained several turtles and she dresses them up for visitors. 3) Padre's shifting sands delight photographers as well as the sunshine and saltwater fanatics.*

The state has a fishing pier here. It is the old causeway between Port Isabel and South Padre Island. The charges are the same as at Port Lavaca and Copano Bay, $1.00 for adults, 50¢ for young people between 13 and 17, and children under 13 free.

The county has two parks on South Padre Island. Camp sites are available for a fee in both Andy Bowie Park and Isla Blanca Park. Isla Blanca Park also has cabanas and overnight shelters for rent.

HIDALGO COUNTY

There were some Spanish settlers a good bit earlier, but Hidalgo County was established as a county in 1852. It includes areas that previously were part of Cameron and Starr counties.

Hidalgo County has some oil and gas production, but the big industry is agriculture. Cotton and citrus, grain and vegetables are big money makers in Hidalgo County. Winter tourists put a lot of money into the economy here, too.

1

1) *Like its neighbors, Hidalgo County benefits from tourism and some oil and gas production. However, vegetables — like these onions — along with grain, fruit and cotton give the county much of its employment and income. 2) The county's courthouse is at Edinburg. It was built in 1955. Edinburg originally was on the Rio Grande, opposite Reynosa. It was moved to where it is now in 1908.*

2

The county was named for the Mexican patriot and revolutionary Father Miguel Hidalgo y Costilla, executed by the Spanish in 1811. Edinburg has been the county seat since the county was founded, but Edinburg has not been in the same place all that time. Edinburg was on the Rio Grande, opposite Reynosa when the county was organized, and it was first designated the county

3

3) *This is the Hidalgo County Historical Museum at Edinburg. The building's stucco exterior is representative of the type of architecture to be found in South Texas cities where Spanish influence remains strong. 4) This was a salt lake two centuries ago and El Sal del Rey provided salt for the area around Hidalgo County when it was a part of Mexico. The court fight over ownership of this salt deposit helped establish Texas mineral law.*

4

seat. Edinburg was moved 14 miles north to the present location in 1908. The present courthouse at Edinburg was built in 1955.

The Hidalgo County Historical Museum at 107 East McIntyre in Edinburg has a collection of momentoes of life in the Hidalgo County area in the early days. The museum is open Wednesday, Saturday and Sunday afternoons. There is a small admission charge.

Old Edinburg became Hidalgo when the new town of Edinburg was established. The old courthouse, jail and post office are still standing in the town now called Hidalgo. They are at

1) Reynosa is just across the Rio Grande River from McAllen. Many tourists cross the border briefly to go through the markets and shops of Reynosa. 2) From McAllen you also can reach the Santa Ana Wildlife Refuge which covers 2,000 acres. The area here is preserved much as it was in the days before "the Valley" became intensively irrigated.

McAllen and 13th. They date from 1886. It is just as well they moved Edinburg away from the river. The Rio Grande changes its channel from time to time and some of what used to be Edinburg is now in or on the other side of the river.

There is another one of those salt lakes the early Spaniards took salt from outside of Linn in the northern end of Hidalgo County. It is El Sal del Rey. The Spaniards and the Mexicans held that all minerals belonged to the state. All the salt in the Kingdom belonged to the King in the Spanish scheme of things. This

3) Mission, Texas, got its name from this early mission, founded by the Oblate Fathers in 1849. It is called La Lomita and it is situated south of the city of Mission on Farm Road 1016. The chapel of the mission is still being used for religious services.

place was a source of the King's salt — El Sal del Rey. The Republic of Texas inherited the Spanish and Mexican claim to mineral rights, but the state of Texas relinquished all mineral rights to property owners in 1866. It was one thing the carpet bag government did that no subsequent government wanted to undo. There was a court fight over ownership of El Sal del Rey, and it played a large part in the development of Texas mineral law.

U. S. Highway 83 through Hidalgo County has been called the longest Main Street in the world. Highway 83 passes through one booming Valley town after another, from Weslaco to Sullivan City. Weslaco is the home of the biggest grapefruit juice plant in the world.

Alamo has a Live Steam Museum. It is two miles north of town on Farm Road 907. It is open daily during the winter months, December to April. Exhibits are old steam engines of various kinds. Donations are welcome.

McAllen is the gateway to Reynosa and the Santa Ana Wildlife Refuge. The refuge covers 2,000 acres. It is an area preserved the way it was before irrigated farming began in the Valley. It is open all day every day. No camping is permitted.

The McAllen International Museum at 2500 Quince Street has exhibits on art and science and history. The museum is open daily except Mondays. There is no charge for admission.

1) *The Bentsen Rio Grande State Park at Mission covers about 600 acres and both camping and picnicking are allowed. There are impressive growths of Spanish moss on many of the old trees.*

There is an old clock museum in Pharr. It is at 927 Preston Street. There are more than 500 timepieces on display here and a lot of information about methods of keeping time. The Old Clock Museum is open daily. There is no charge for admission.

Mission is the home of the Texas ruby red grapefruit. The Bentsen Rio Grande State Park is on the river at Mission. The park covers nearly 600 acres. There are provisions for camping and picnicking. Fishing is permitted. This is one of the state's Class I parks, so the admission fee of $1.00 per vehicle applies unless you have an annual permit.

A marker at Bryan and North Mission Street in Mission attests that William Jennings Bryan was one of the early winter visitors to this part of the Valley. Bryan bought property here in 1910 and spent two winters in a home that still stands here. The mission the town of Mission was named for is La Lomita. It was built by the Oblate Fathers in 1849 and the chapel is still in use. La Lomita is south of Mission on Farm Road 1016.

There are several places to cross the Rio Grande into Mexico, and there is something to see and do at Matamoros and Reynosa.

If you cross at Los Ebanos, there is nothing to do on the other side, unless you want to rent a donkey and ride to the cantina. The crossing itself is the experience here. The ferryboat is one of the old ones. You cross the same way the pioneers crossed the rivers before bridges. Los Ebanos ferry crossing is on Farm Road 886, south of U. S. 83. It will help you appreciate how far we have come. It may even make you appreciate the freeways.

2

2) The ferry at Los Ebanos is a survivor from the days when ferries were anything but elegant. The crew manipulates ropes to get the ferry from one side of the river to the other in much the same way ferries operated generations ago. The crossing is on Farm Road 886, south of U.S. 83. 3) The Gulf of Mexico has been a commercial blessing to development of Texas, giving it a highway to the world. In more recent times, the Gulf has brought a growing army of sun, sand and fishing enthusiasts to the state's shores. But it has extracted a price too, as attested by the remains of boats and ships that wash ashore on the lower coast particularly after fall storms. The Coast Guard makes a continuing effort to educate private boat owners to the need for training and caution when going offshore.

3

Sabine River

Beaumont ●
Sabine lighthouse ★

Baytown ●

Houston ●

*Bolivar Point
lighthouse* ★
Port Bolivar ★
Galveston
Galveston lighthouse

El Campo ●

Point Comfort
Victoria ●
Point Comfort lighthouse ★
Port Lavaca
★ *Matagorda lighthouse*
Lavaca Bay
Pass Cavallo

GULF OF MEXICO

★ *Aransas Pass lighthouse*
Aransas Pass

Corpus Christi ●

Kingsville ●

N

★ *Port Isabel lighthouse*
● Port Isabel
● Brownsville

The Lighthouses of the Coast

There once were 15 lighthouses on the Texas coast. Most of them are gone now. All the lighthouse keepers are gone. The few lights still in service are automated, and most navigators use electronics more than lighthouses.

One of the surviving lighthouses is one of the smallest state parks in Texas. This is the Point Isabel Lighthouse at Port Isabel.

The Point Isabel Lighthouse was built in 1852 on a site General Zachary Taylor had used as a fort during the Mexican War. It was discovered about 1888 that the government never had bothered to acquire the land Taylor was using for his fort. The lighthouse was on private property. The owner and the government argued about it for a while, and the government finally bought the land and the lighthouse in 1894 for $6,000.

The light was taken out of commission early in the 20th Century. The State Parks Department acquired the lighthouse and one acre of land later. The lighthouse is one of the Texas landmarks most often photographed. It is still in good condition, and it is open to visitors. It is the only lighthouse in Texas that is.

The lighthouse built at Aransas Pass in 1855 is still standing. But it has been out of service for a long time, and it is in private hands. The owner is H. E. Butt of the grocery chain.

A lighthouse was built on Half Moon Reef in Matagorda Bay in 1858. This one was taken out of service about 1888, and it was later moved to Point Comfort. It is in reasonably good condition and it is standing now on the north side of State Highway 35 near the Lavaca Bay Bridge in Point Comfort. It may eventually be moved to the park in Port Lavaca and put on display.

The Matagorda Lighthouse was built in 1852 at the entrance to Matagorda Bay. The tower is cast iron. It was damaged and neglected during the Civil War and it was rebuilt in 1873 on the west side of Pass Cavallo. This site is about two miles from the original site, and the lighthouse is still standing and still in use. It was automated in 1956.

There have been several lights and lightships at and around Galveston and in Galveston Bay. The one now standing at the end of the Galveston jetty is one built in 1918. Construction started originally in 1905, but the job was delayed twice by hurricanes. This lighthouse is still working.

The lighthouse at Bolivar Point is just like the Matagorda Lighthouse. This one has been rebuilt, too, since it was established in 1852. The Confederates dismantled this lighthouse during the Civil War and used the cast iron plates for something else.

This tower was completed in 1872. More than 100 people took shelter here during the great hurricane of 1900. Several dozen people rode out the hurricane of 1915 here.

The Bolivar Point Lighthouse was taken out of service in 1933. It and the two keepers' cottages are now private property. The property is right alongside State Highway 87 at Port Bolivar.

The Sabine Lighthouse at the mouth of the Sabine-Neches Waterway is actually on the Louisiana coast, on the east side of the Sabine. This one was built in 1856. It remained in service until the 1950s. This picture was made shortly after a grass fire had destroyed the keepers' houses.

The buttresses at the base of the Sabine Lighthouse resemble rocket fins. From the Texas side of the river, the thing looks a little like a rocket crouched on a launching pad.

1) When the U.S. Government built this lighthouse in 1852 it cost only $7,000 intended to aid commerce on the Rio Grande. Several battles were fought o lighthouse during the Civil War since both sides considered it an excellent l point. It continued as a sentinel tower until 1943 when it was declared uns use. It is now a state historic site.

ORT ISABEL LIGHTHOUSE STATE PARK
TEXAS PARKS & WILDLIFE DEPARTMENT

1

1

1) This lighthouse at Aransas Pass still appears to be in good condition. It was b
1855 and has not seen service as a lighthouse for decades. It is in private hands,
owned by a grocery chain operator. 2) Matagorda's lighthouse, built in 1852
entrance to Matagorda Bay, was damaged during the Civil War and was no
maintained after the war. It was rebuilt in 1873 on the west side of Pass Cavalle
miles from where it was to start with. It is one of the few Texas lighthouse
operating.

1

1) *This lighthouse was built in 1858 on Half Moon Reef in Matagorda Bay. It*
service 30 years before being moved to Point Comfort. It stands now near the
Bay Bridge. Having survived more than a century of the worst weather th
could aim at it, the old building may eventually be moved to Port Lavaca for r
tion and display purposes. 2) Standing at the end of Galveston's long jett
lighthouse is still in use on an automated basis. It was started in 1905 but u
completed until 1918 because of interference from several hurricanes.

2

e Bolivar Point lighthouse is now in private hands and is not in service as a
itional aid. It has a long history, however, of helping mariners and those on
as well. It was built first in 1852. Confederate forces tore the original tower
during the Civil War to salvage the iron plates. The present tower was com-
in 1872 and it served as a place of shelter for Bolivar residents during the great
anes of 1900 and 1915. It was taken out of service in 1933. 2) The Sabine
ouse at the mouth of the Sabine-Neches Waterway, since it is on the east side of
annel, technically is in Louisiana. It was built in 1856 and remained in service
out a century.

1) *The extinct lighthouse at Aransas Pass now looks out mostly on seagulls and fishermen. In their 19th Century heyday, such towers were lifesavers for seamen. There was no scientific storm warning system like we have today and mariners seldom knew when a storm or hurricane might overtake them. The beacons on shore could make the difference between life and death for a ship's crew fighting temper-mental Gulf weather.*

Photo Credits

All photographs for this book, with the exception of those listed below, were taken by Ray Miller, Gary James or Bob Brandon of the "Eyes of Texas" program, KPRC-TV, Houston, or by Mark Williams. The authors and publisher wish to express their appreciation to the following people and organizations for allowing the reproduction of photographs from their collections.

The first number of each entry signifies the page on which the borrowed photograph appears. The second number indicates its numerical reference on the page. For example: 3-2 indicates the photograph is found on page 3 and is referenced by the numeral 2 on that page.

Brazos River Harbor Navigation District: 66-3
Confederate Air Force, Harlingen: 172-1
Diamond M Company: 128-1
Ray D. Edmondson: 17-2, 17-3
First National Bank of Freeport: 136-1
Charles W. Fisher Jr.: 9-3
Fort Bend County Museum, Richmond: 74-2, 75-4
Clyde Gray's Heritage Village, Woodville: 8-1, 18-1
Houston Chamber of Commerce: 80-1
Houston Public Library: 113-4, 144-1
Sam Houston Regional Library, Liberty: 3-2, 3-3, 4-1, 4-3, 5-4, 12-1, 13-3, 22-1
La Retema Library, Corpus Christi: 129-4
Museum of Fine Arts, Bayou Bend Collection, Houston: 88-1, 88-2
NASA: 95-2, 95-3
Rosenberg Library, Galveston: 45-5, 46-1, 46-2, 51-3
Texas State Archives: 78-2
U.S. Navy: 31-3
Victoria Public Library: 106-2, 115-2

Index

Boldface type represents the location of a related photograph.

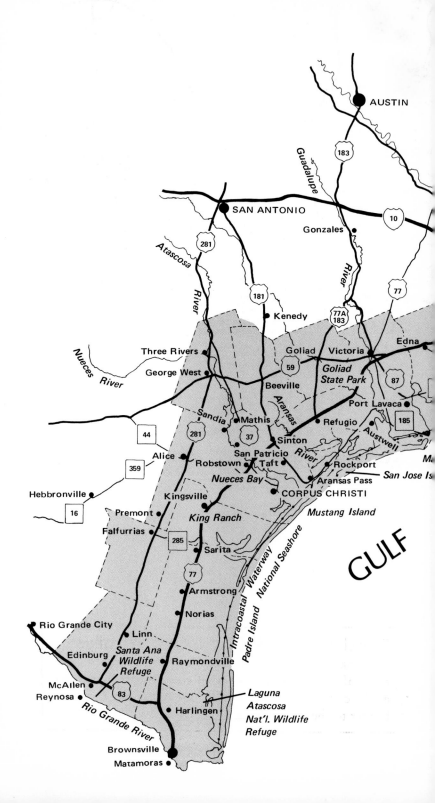

MEXICO

SCALE OF MILES: One inch = 41 miles.
This map encompasses the area covered by the six sections of this book. It covers 30 counties of what is generally called the Texas Gulf Coast, from the Louisiana border to the tip of Texas at Brownsville.